New Daylight

Edited by Naomi Starkey   May–August 2010

Suggestions for using *New Daylight*

Find a regular time and place, if possible, where you can read and pray undisturbed. Before you begin, take time to be still and perhaps use the BRF prayer. Then read the Bible passage slowly (try reading it aloud if you find it over-familiar), followed by the comment. You can also use *New Daylight* for group study and discussion, if you prefer.

The prayer or point for reflection can be a starting point for your own meditation and prayer. Many people like to keep a journal to record their thoughts about a Bible passage and items for prayer. In *New Daylight* we also note the Sundays and some special festivals from the Church calendar, to keep in step with the Christian year.

New Daylight and the Bible

New Daylight contributors use a range of Bible versions, and you will find a list of the versions used in each issue at the back of the notes on page 154. You are welcome to use your own preferred version alongside the passage printed in the notes, and this can be particularly helpful if the Bible text has been abridged.

New Daylight affirms that the whole of the Bible is God's revelation to us, and we should read, reflect on and learn from every part of both Old and New Testaments. Usually the printed comment presents a straight-forward 'thought for the day', but sometimes it may also raise questions rather than simply providing answers, as we wrestle with some of the more difficult passages of Scripture.

New Daylight *is also available in a deluxe edition (larger format). Check out your local Christian bookshop or contact the BRF office, who can also give more details about a cassette version for the visually impaired. For a Braille edition, contact St John's Guild, 8 St Raphael's Court, Avenue Road, St Albans, AL1 3EH.*

Writers in this issue

Helen Julian CSF has written several books for BRF, most recently *The Road to Emmaus*. She is an Anglican Franciscan sister, and presently serves her community as Minister Provincial.

Amy Boucher Pye is an American who has lived in the UK for over a decade. She makes her home in North London with her husband and young family and enjoys writing for Christian periodicals, including *Quiet Spaces*, *Woman Alive* and *Christian Marketplace*.

David Winter is retired from parish ministry. An honorary Canon of Christ Church, Oxford, he is well known as a writer and broadcaster. His most recent book for BRF is *Pilgrim's Way*.

Tony Horsfall is a freelance trainer and retreat leader based in Yorkshire, with his own ministry, Charis Training. He is an elder of Ackworth Community Church and has written several books for BRF, including *Mentoring for Spiritual Growth* and *Working from a Place of Rest*.

Steve Aisthorpe lives in Scotland with his wife and two sons. He is a Development Officer for the Church of Scotland, encouraging mission and discipleship throughout the Highlands and Islands. He was previously Executive Director of the International Nepal Fellowship.

Veronica Zundel is an Oxford graduate, writer and journalist. She lives with her husband and son in North London, where they belong to the Mennonite Church.

Margaret Silf is an ecumenical Christian, committed to working across and beyond the denominational divides. She devotes herself to writing and accompanying others on their spiritual journey.

John Proctor is married to Elaine, with an adult daughter and son. He works for the United Reformed Church, teaching the New Testament in Cambridge and around the church. John has written *The People's Bible Commentary: Matthew* (BRF, 2001) and booklets on the Gospels and Acts in the Grove Biblical Series.

David Robertson has ministered in a variety of parishes since his ordination in 1979 and is currently a vicar in Halifax. He has written *Marriage—Restoring Our Vision* and *Collaborative Ministry* for BRF.

Further BRF reading for this issue

For more in-depth coverage of some of the passages in these Bible reading notes, we recommend the following titles:

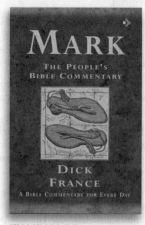

978 1 84101 046 5, £8.99

978 1 84101 118 9, £7.99

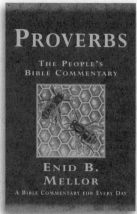

978 1 84101 071 7, £7.99

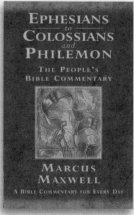

978 1 84101 047 2, £7.99

Naomi Starkey writes...

If you have already flicked through this latest copy of *New Daylight*, you may have spotted a difference! If you have instead turned straight to this page to read the editor's letter (I flatter myself...), you may like to take a moment to scan the rest of the issue. Notice anything? The comment is now set out in a single column—as the Bible passage is already—rather than two narrow columns as in the past.

We have made this change partly to refresh the look of the notes and partly because having a longer line on the page slows down the eye, so that the comment can be read more reflectively. The old two-column layout had the feel of a traditional newspaper column—the sort of material that we tend to skim rather than read at a leisurely pace. Having a single column also makes the text easier to deliver by email, as these days an increasing number of people prefer to download their reading—or music—on to some kind of mobile device.

If you are interested in finding out more about receiving *New Daylight* by email, either for yourself or for somebody you know, you can visit www.biblereadingnotes.org.uk/862 for more information.

Also in this issue, we begin what will be a regular feature: 11 June, the festival of Barnabas the Apostle, will be a chance to remember BRF's Barnabas children's ministry in some way. The Barnabas team go regularly into schools and churches around the UK to provide teaching days and other special events to help children on their spiritual journey, while the Barnabas range of books offers lively resources for children and those working with children. In recent years, the ministry has gone from strength to strength, particularly through the Messy Church initiative, and I am delighted to have the regular opportunity to remind *New Daylight* readers of the breadth of BRF's work.

Finally, I'd like once again to thank all the readers who have written or emailed to let us know how they have found the notes—the topics and contributors they enjoyed and also what they didn't enjoy (and it is always helpful to hear why). We take our readers' views very seriously and endeavour to take on board in some way the comments and suggestions we receive. Carry on keeping in touch!

The BRF Prayer

Almighty God,

you have taught us that your word is a lamp for our feet
and a light for our path. Help us, and all who prayerfully
read your word, to deepen our fellowship with each other
through your love. And in so doing may we come to know you more
fully, love you more truly, and follow more faithfully in
the steps of your son Jesus Christ, who lives and reigns with
you and the Holy Spirit, one God for evermore. Amen.

Snapshots of Jesus in Mark

In the second of our series of 'Gospel snapshots', we turn to a section of Mark's Gospel, which is probably the earliest of the four Gospels and also the shortest and most fast-paced. We get a good flavour of the writer's approach from the chapters we consider. Jesus is perpetually on the move: there are quick cuts from scene to scene, from place to place, and the Gospel writer often uses the word 'immediately'.

Although we hear of Jesus teaching his disciples and other followers, we don't often hear what he was teaching—at least, not in words. His teaching comes primarily through his actions, as it does in the first and last of the stories that we read in this section of the Gospel. In the first of them we see also another characteristic of Mark's Gospel—the opposition that Jesus faces and the dialogues with those who oppose him.

These aspects aside, there are also some more traditional teachings recorded and they are to be found in these chapters. They are in the form of parables—those intriguing but often obscure stories that frequently baffled their first hearers and still have the power to intrigue and baffle today.

It's easy to misunderstand the parable form; often we treat them as allegories, in which every item must represent something. The parable of the sower, for example, which falls within these chapters, has been interpreted by the Gospel writer as an allegory, with each kind of seed standing for a particular response to the gospel. Most commentators, however, agree that Jesus taught only the actual parable and the explanation has been added by the evangelist.

Parables, in contrast to allegories, are self-contained stories that, as a whole story, contain the point. We need to learn to look at them in this way and not expect every element within them to mean something. Similarly, when we look at a great painting, we can examine every detail and wonder at the craftsmanship, but if we never stand back and look at the picture as a whole, we miss the overall experience.

The parables need to be lived with, ruminated on, allowed to work on us, rather than being analysed and perhaps too easily explained. In this they are particularly pointed examples of all Jesus' teaching—teaching that is meant to draw us into the strange new life of the kingdom.

Helen Julian CSF

Law and grace

Again [Jesus] entered the synagogue, and a man was there who had a withered hand. They watched him to see whether he would cure him on the sabbath, so that they might accuse him. And he said to the man who had the withered hand, 'Come forward.' Then he said to them, 'Is it lawful to do good or to do harm on the sabbath, to save life or to kill?' But they were silent. He looked around at them with anger; he was grieved at their hardness of heart and said to the man, 'Stretch out your hand.' He stretched it out, and his hand was restored. The Pharisees went out and immediately conspired with the Herodians against him, how to destroy him.

This is the last of five stories in which Jesus comes into conflict with the religious authorities. By the end of it, their opposition has become overt and potentially violent. Each of the five takes place in a different setting as Jesus is constantly on the move, preaching his good news and doing the works of God in every corner of his world.

This miracle, with its attendant teaching, takes place in the synagogue Jesus goes to regularly—the word 'again' at the start of the passage tells us that. In Mark's Gospel, however, it becomes a place of opposition and he records only one further visit (6:1–6), during which Jesus is rejected by his own people. Jesus' question about the legality of healing on the sabbath is a complex one. Even the Pharisees, with their strict adherence to the law, would have made an exception in order to save life. The man's withered hand was not a life-threatening condition, however, so could have been healed on another day.

Sabbath observance had become a weapon, a means to separate people into the righteous and the unrighteous, rather than a celebration of God's creation and redemption of the whole world. Jesus, in his blatant violation of this part of the law, was insisting on a higher imperative and demonstrating that God's redeeming and healing power cannot be confined by human laws.

Reflection

Are there times when today's Church puts rule-keeping above enabling and welcoming the healing and restorative work of God among his people?

HJ CSF

Called and sent

[Jesus] went up the mountain and called to him those whom he wanted, and they came to him. And he appointed twelve, whom he also named apostles, to be with him, and to be sent out to proclaim the message, and to have authority to cast out demons. So he appointed the twelve: Simon (to whom he gave the name Peter); James son of Zebedee and John the brother of James (to whom he gave the name Boanerges, that is, Sons of Thunder); and Andrew, and Philip, and Bartholomew, and Matthew, and Thomas, and James son of Alphaeus, and Thaddaeus, and Simon the Cananaean, and Judas Iscariot, who betrayed him.

This is a marvellous passage to accompany reflection on discipleship. We can easily see the apostles as 'supermen', doing amazing deeds of power, preaching the good news and often suffering and dying for it. This is indeed part of their story, but, primarily, they were called to 'be with' Jesus and only then 'to be sent out to proclaim the message'.

The place of their calling is significant. Traditionally in the Bible, mountains are places of encounter with God (think of Moses and Elijah). The particular 'mountain' referred to here is in fact the hills around Lake Galilee, which were known as a place for plotting revolution. They were the place to which the disaffected withdrew, to plan the overthrow of the hated Roman colonial power. In going to this place, Mark is pointing up the revolutionary nature of Jesus' mission. Also, his choice of twelve apostles clearly refers to the twelve tribes of Israel and so to a promise of restoration, the fulfilment of the prophets' words.

The fact that we have the names (although in the other Gospels some of the names are different) shows that discipleship is individual—about this particular person and that one. The fact that not all of those listed became well-known, important figures in the early Church makes it more likely that this passage reflects reality rather than being added later to give legitimacy to the Church's leaders. It speaks also to our own discipleship, which may well be one of obscurity.

Prayer

Jesus, may I be with you and do your work in obscurity or prominence.

HJ CSF

Whose is the power?

Then [Jesus] went home; and the crowd came together again, so that they could not even eat. When his family heard it, they went out to restrain him, for people were saying, 'He has gone out of his mind.' And the scribes who came down from Jerusalem said, 'He has Beelzebul, and by the ruler of the demons he casts out demons.' And he called them to him, and spoke to them in parables, 'How can Satan cast out Satan? If a kingdom is divided against itself, that kingdom cannot stand. And if a house is divided against itself, that house will not be able to stand. And if Satan has risen up against himself and is divided, he cannot stand, but his end has come.'

This must have been one of the most hurtful of all the experiences of rejection for Jesus. His own family is inclined to believe those who think that he is mad and, further, come out to try and prevent him from bringing any more shame on them by his activities. I wonder if Mary—who had (in Luke's Gospel) been made aware of God's purpose in his birth and life and death—was with them?

The scribes from Jerusalem were the fully official representatives of the Jewish faith, so their words would have been taken very seriously by the crowds. Interestingly, they didn't deny that Jesus was doing powerful works; they only questioned the source of his supernatural power. Also, they had come some way to do this, so clearly Jesus' fame had spread even to Jerusalem and his activities were being seen as a threat.

Jesus points out that the results of his work are the polar opposite of the work of Satan. If he was indeed doing the work of Satan and not the work of God, then Satan would be pursuing two conflicting agendas at once and his end would be near.

Mark is unique in using 'Beelzebul' as an alternative name for Satan. It is found as 'Baal-zebub', the name of a Philistine god, in 2 Kings 1:2 and is thought to have meant 'Lord of the house', thus bringing an extra layer of meaning to Jesus' words about a house divided against itself. Any house, any kingdom, can have only one Lord.

Reflection
Who or what is Lord in my life?

HJ CSF

Ears to hear, eyes to see

[Jesus] said to them, 'Is a lamp brought in to be put under the bushel basket, or under the bed, and not on the lampstand? For there is nothing hidden, except to be disclosed; nor is anything secret, except to come to light. Let anyone with ears to hear listen!' And he said to them, 'Pay attention to what you hear; the measure you give will be the measure you get, and still more will be given you. For to those who have, more will be given; and from those who have nothing, even what they have will be taken away.'

Between the last passage and this comes the well-known parable of the sower, with its explanation of the meaning of the seeds falling in various places. Although it is likely that only the parable itself was actually spoken by Jesus and the explanation was added by the evangelist, it is a model of clarity compared to the few verses of our passage today.

In fact, there are five or perhaps six separate sayings—all also found in different contexts in the Gospels of Matthew and Luke—that Mark has combined to form a pair of related parables, on the basis of the similar subject matter or even the coincidence of related vocabulary. The word translated as 'bushel' in the first parable really means a two-gallon measure and therefore links to the 'measure' of the second parable.

Mark had to decide where to put these two new parables and chose here because he has interpreted them as referring to the temporary concealment of the news of the kingdom by means of Jesus' teaching in parables. Given all the complexity involved in their genesis, it is impossible to be sure of their original meaning, but this does not mean that they have nothing to teach us and, indeed, commentators suggest various interpretations.

Tom Wright in his commentary sees them both in the light of promise and warning. The first promises that the kingdom message will soon be public knowledge, so pay attention now because you will need to know! The second promises that paying attention will enable God to give the hearer more, but those who continue to live at a superficial level will lose even what they presently have.

Prayer
Lord, give me ears to hear and a heart to receive.

HJ CSF

God gives the growth

[Jesus] also said, 'The kingdom of God is as if someone would scatter seed on the ground, and would sleep and rise night and day, and the seed would sprout and grow, he does not know how. The earth produces of itself, first the stalk, then the head, then the full grain in the head. But when the grain is ripe, at once he goes in with his sickle, because the harvest has come.' He also said, 'With what can we compare the kingdom of God, or what parable will we use for it? It is like a mustard seed, which, when sown upon the ground, is the smallest of all the seeds on earth; yet when it is sown it grows up and becomes the greatest of all shrubs, and puts forth large branches, so that the birds of the air can make nests in its shade.'

The opposition Jesus was facing must have been discouraging for his disciples, so perhaps these two parables were given to encourage them.

The first is found only in Mark, and is a good counterbalance to the belief that hard work on our part will accomplish everything we want. All that the farmer in the parable does is scatter the seed, then go about his life. He doesn't hover anxiously over it.

We might see this as a parable of the steady growth of the kingdom, but that is a modern idea. Jesus taught that it was coming soon and in unexpected ways. God gives his gifts in his time, not as a result of us working our way to redemption, step by careful step. 'The earth produces of itself' is a very emphatic phrase in the Greek. Perhaps it can help us when we feel impatient or discouraged.

The second parable may have been given to encourage the small band of disciples with its teaching that something great can come from small and insignificant beginnings. My own religious community, as did most others, began with a very small number of people, but God used that small beginning to create a community now over 100 years old. It is easy to get caught up in the numbers culture, where more is always better. We should never forget that small can be beautiful, too!

Reflection

Do either of these parables speak to areas of discouragement in my life?

HJ CSF

God of the storms

On that day, when evening had come, [Jesus] said to [his disciples], 'Let us go across to the other side.'... A great gale arose, and the waves beat into the boat, so that the boat was already being swamped. But he was in the stern, asleep on the cushion; and they woke him up and said to him, 'Teacher, do you not care that we are perishing?' He woke up and rebuked the wind, and said to the sea, 'Peace! Be still!' Then the wind ceased, and there was a dead calm. He said to them, 'Why are you afraid? Have you still no faith?' And they were filled with great awe and said to one another, 'Who then is this, that even the wind and the sea obey him?'

Our reading of this story gains greater depth from a knowledge of the Old Testament background. Creation had involved God in a contest with the forces of evil and chaos, identified with the waters of the oceans. Therefore, the ability to control the sea was a sign of divine power (Psalm 89:8–9; Isaiah 51:9–10). Indeed, the image of stormy waters was often used as a metaphor for the evil forces active in the world, especially for all that afflicted the righteous—tribulations in which only the power of God could save them (Psalm 69:1–2, 14–15). Confidence in the face of even the most terrible storm came to be used as an image of complete confidence in God, who had the power and the will to save (Psalm 46:1–3; Isaiah 43:2). Also, the ability to sleep peacefully was a sign of perfect trust in God (Leviticus 26:6; Job 11:18–19; Proverbs 3:23–24).

Therefore the early hearers of this story would experience not only a story about a wonder worker but also one about someone in whom the power of God was living and acting, an agent of God, if not God himself. The disciples' fearful response strengthens this reading of the story. In the Old Testament, fear is often a response to the presence of God, but here God is also one on whom they can call: 'do you not care that we are perishing?' Mark also leaves us with the question 'Who then is this…?'

Reflection
How do you answer Mark's question?

HJ CSF

Healing and salvation

Then one of the leaders of the synagogue named Jairus came and, when he saw him, fell at his feet and begged him repeatedly, 'My little daughter is at the point of death. Come and lay your hands on her, so that she may be made well, and live.' So he went with him... Some people came from the leader's house to say, 'Your daughter is dead. Why trouble the teacher any further?' But overhearing what they said, Jesus said to the leader of the synagogue, 'Do not fear, only believe.'... When they came to the house of the leader of the synagogue, he saw a commotion, people weeping and wailing loudly.

The disciples have been challenged to have faith in Jesus in the midst of a storm. Now, in the story of Jairus' daughter, we have someone whose faith is tested by one of the most severe 'storms' of human life—the death of someone we love. Fear and faith battle it out.

In Mark's Gospel, the synagogue is a place of controversy and conflict, but Jairus is willing to step outside his official position, perhaps making himself suspect in the eyes of the religious authorities, in order to save his daughter. We don't know whether he was already a believer or whether this was a desperate last attempt to save his daughter, perhaps out of a sense of having nothing to lose. Certainly not all his household were convinced of Jesus' powers and we might well be with them. We might be willing to believe in the healing of someone gravely sick, but that anyone can raise the dead—no, that is beyond possibility.

The words used by Jairus in his request—'that she may be made well, and live'—in fact contain both possibilities within them as they can also be translated to mean 'that she may be saved and attain (eternal) life'. Healing and salvation are very closely linked in biblical thought. Our prayers for healing for ourselves or others may not always be answered with physical recovery from illness, but salvation is always held out to us and that is the faith which can overcome fear.

Prayer

Healer, Saviour, make me willing to set aside my dignity and to come to you for healing and salvation.

HJ CSF

MARK 5:39–43 (NRSV, ABRIDGED)

Wakening to life

When [Jesus] had entered, he said to them, 'Why do you make a commotion and weep? The child is not dead but sleeping.' And they laughed at him. Then he put them all outside, and took the child's father and mother and those who were with him, and went in where the child was. He took her by the hand and said to her, 'Talitha cum', which means, 'Little girl, get up!' And immediately the girl got up and began to walk about... At this they were overcome with amazement. He strictly ordered them that no one should know this, and told them to give her something to eat.

Jesus arrives at Jairus' house, where his quiet assurance contrasts vividly with the frenzied weeping of the mourners. 'Sleep' was a common euphemism for death in the ancient world, but the Christian readers would have heard it differently. The dead were described as 'sleeping' because they would one day be awakened. So, when Jesus speaks to the child, he uses the words ordinarily used to waken a daughter in the morning: 'Time to get up, little girl!'

Jesus and his disciples probably spoke Aramaic and these are some of the few words recorded in that language in the Gospels. They are very ordinary words—not religious or magical, just words that would have been heard in many households every morning. God breaks in through ordinary words and events and does something extraordinary.

The raising of this child is a foretaste of what Jesus promises to everyone who believes. He brings forward from eternity into history the awakening that is his gift to all. Not surprisingly, this has a shattering impact on those who witness it. The words used to describe their amazement are unusually strong. Nicholas King SJ translates them as 'They were beside themselves with great ecstasy'.

To confirm the reality of this great inbreaking of eternal life into the temporal world, Jesus tells them to give her something to eat. It may remind us of Jesus on the beach after his own resurrection, cooking for his disciples and eating with them. Resurrection life is real life.

Reflection
What in you needs to be brought back to life?

HJ CSF

Mark 5:25–30, 33–34 (NRSV, abridged)

Touching Jesus

Now there was a woman who had been suffering from haem-
orrhages for twelve years. She had endured much under many
physicians... and she was no better, but rather grew worse. She
had heard about Jesus, and came up behind him in the crowd and
touched his cloak, for she said, 'If I but touch his clothes, I will
be made well.' Immediately her haemorrhage stopped; and she
felt in her body that she was healed of her disease. Immediately
aware that power had gone forth from him, Jesus turned about
in the crowd and said, 'Who touched my clothes?'... The woman,
knowing what had happened to her, came in fear and trembling...
and told him the whole truth. He said to her, 'Daughter, your faith
has made you well; go in peace, and be healed of your disease.'

In this final 'snapshot' from Mark's Gospel, Jesus encounters a woman
who, because of her bleeding, was a source of impurity. For her, what
afflicted all women for a time each month was a permanent state. It
would have isolated her socially: she was not supposed to be in the
crowd as she put any who touched her at risk of sharing her ritual
impurity. She is desperate, though, like Jairus, and so risks discovery
and humiliation to draw close to Jesus. Like Jairus, pleading for his
daughter, she is seeking both healing and salvation.

Initially she is 'made well' by the power that flows from Jesus, but
it is only after her face-to-face encounter with him and her declaration
of faith in him that she is also 'healed'—that is, 'saved'. Jesus' power
and her faith are both needed to bring about this change, but it is her
touch and his awareness of it that spark the intimate encounter. Jesus'
addressing of her as 'daughter' shows that what has occurred between
them has brought her into a close personal relationship with him.

As in the first of our stories in this section of Mark, Jesus disregards
the law in order to do God's work. There he broke the sabbath law; here
he breaks through the laws of ritual purity and impurity. The imperative
to bring healing and salvation is greater than the law.

Prayer

Jesus, may I draw close to you, touch you and be touched by you—
today and always.

HJ CSF

Ephesians: the riches of Christ

The apostle Paul's letter to the Ephesians may be relatively short, but it has shaped the lives of countless Christians. Some have called it the crown of Paul's letters; others say that, 'pound for pound', it is the most influential document ever written.

Paul may have intended for churches throughout Asia Minor to read it, not just the church at Ephesus (in modern-day Turkey) for it is less personal than his other letters and he does not address specific concerns and heresies. Rather, Paul outlines God's cosmic plan of redemption through his Son, Jesus Christ, then gives the new believers instructions on how to live.

The first part is a song of praise for Christ and how God has revealed to Paul the amazing mystery of our (that is, the Gentiles') salvation through him. God has lavished his grace on us through Christ and has sealed us with the Holy Spirit. We are now heirs of his glorious riches.

Paul then explores the old life versus the new, urging the believers to dwell in Christ, leaving their old selves behind, for Christ has shattered the former divisions between peoples and races and calls for a life of unity and peace. No longer are we foreigners and strangers, but citizens and members of God's household. Now we dwell in Christ, being rooted and established in him.

If the first half of Paul's letter is cosmic, theological and lofty, the second half is deeply practical. Paul gives instructions for unity and maturity, urging the believers to live a life worthy of the calling that they have received. No longer should we give ourselves over to drunkenness or debauchery; we should be filled with the Holy Spirit. As we put on our new selves, we take on the virtues of humility, love, patience, grace, holiness and kindness. We submit to each other out of love for Christ.

At the end of Paul's letter, he calls believers to action. He urges us to put on the armour of God so as to stand firm in the battle that rages around us, namely in the heavenly realms. As we arm ourselves with his resources, we will be able to stand up to anything.

As you engage with the riches of Paul's letter, may you receive the power, together with all the Lord's people, to grasp how wide and long and high and deep is the love of Christ.

Amy Boucher Pye

In Christ

Praise be to the God and Father of our Lord Jesus Christ, who has blessed us in the heavenly realms with every spiritual blessing in Christ. For he chose us in him before the creation of the world to be holy and blameless in his sight… In him we have redemption through his blood, the forgiveness of sins, in accordance with the riches of God's grace that he lavished on us… In him we were also chosen, having been predestined… in order that we, who were the first to put our hope in Christ, might be for the praise of his glory. And you also were included in Christ when you heard the word of truth, the gospel of your salvation.

In the Greek, Ephesians 1:3–14 is all one sentence, forming Paul's expression of praise for what God has done through his Son, Jesus Christ. Repeated throughout these verses is the phrase 'in Christ'. In the Greek, it appears eleven times and, in the whole of Ephesians, 36 times. In Paul's writings overall, it shows up 164 times. Many biblical commentators, including Klyne Snodgrass, author of *The NIV Application Commentary: Ephesians*, refer to this theme as Paul's central theological idea.

What does it mean to be 'in Christ'? We see various meanings here: God chose us in Christ to be his children; through Christ we are redeemed and forgiven; we are to hope in Christ; through him we believe. We are in Christ and he is in us; we are joined with him and have union with him.

This oneness with Christ changes us from the inside out. It is mystical, for this is the realm of the unseen invading our lives. It is practical, too, for, as we dwell in him, we find the resources to live in his way. That could mean speaking up for the poor, joyfully making a cup of tea for a builder, spending time with someone who is housebound, reining in our tongues or spreading peace and love with those we meet. Christ defines us and our understanding of reality. He truly is our 'all in all'.

Prayer

Lord Jesus Christ, I find my identity in you. Fill me with your presence this day, that your love, grace and truth might overflow from within.

ABP

The riches of our hope

Ever since I heard about your faith in the Lord Jesus and your love for all his people, I have not stopped giving thanks for you, remembering you in my prayers. I keep asking that the God of our Lord Jesus Christ, the glorious Father, may give you the Spirit of wisdom and revelation, so that you may know him better. I pray that the eyes of your heart may be enlightened in order that you may know the hope to which he has called you, the riches of his glorious inheritance in his people, and his incomparably great power for us who believe.

Paul moves from praise to a prayer of intercession and thanksgiving for his readers. He longs that they will know Christ better through the Holy Spirit's wisdom, revelation and enlightenment. He uses wonderfully imaginative language when he prays for the opening of the eyes of their hearts and he prays that they will receive God's hope, riches and power.

When we are grounded in Christ, we are filled with hope. Theologian C.F.D. Moule has a marvellous definition for this Christian virtue, namely 'faith standing on tiptoe' (as quoted in *The NIV Application Commentary*). Our circumstances may seem unrelenting or impenetrable, but we can ask God to stretch our faith and give us the hope to believe his promises.

When my much-loved publishing job was eliminated a few years ago, my first reaction was pain and disbelief. I turned to God, asking him to fill me with hope for the future. The loss didn't disappear instantly, but gradually chinks of light appeared in the darkness. Over time I have, with God's help, been able to form a lifestyle that affords me more time with my small children, along with enriching writing and editing.

Have you lost hope? If the waters seem to be washing over you, may you be able to grasp the Lord's life raft today. May he bring you encouragement, whether through a verse of scripture leaping off the page, the assurance of his never-ending love, the laughter of children, the caress of a loved one or, perhaps, even a new job prospect.

Prayer

'Be strong and take heart, all you who hope in the Lord' (Psalm 31:24).

ABP

The message of salvation

You were dead in your transgressions and sins, in which you used to live when you followed the ways of this world and of the ruler of the kingdom of the air... All of us also lived among them at one time, gratifying the cravings of our sinful nature and following its desires and thoughts... But because of his great love for us, God, who is rich in mercy, made us alive with Christ even when we were dead in transgressions... For it is by grace you have been saved, through faith—and this is not from yourselves, it is the gift of God—not by works, so that no one can boast. For we are God's handiwork, created in Christ Jesus to do good works.

Some say that Ephesians 2:1–10 is the best biblical summary of the gospel. In the previous chapter, Paul talks of an exultation of God through Christ on a cosmic level, but here he turns to the level of humanity, showing how God has saved us from our sinful lives. He compares the old with the new: once we were dead, but now we are alive; once we were ruled by the cravings of our flesh, but now we are saved.

This is all the result of pure grace. God in his mercy pulls us out of the graves we dig for ourselves, through lies, slander, bitterness, unbelief or unforgiveness. He releases us from the tangles of these deathly cords and sets us on a solid foundation. When we are placed firmly on the rock of Christ, we are then propelled into a life of good works. Lest we claim this goodness for ourselves, Paul reminds us that these works, too, are a gift from God. We are God's craftsmanship, his handiwork, his workmanship; in short, we are his works of art. Fuelled by grace, we find joy in the release from our sinful nature.

Some people have amazing conversion stories, turning to Christ from a life of drugs, sex or the occult. Others, like me, have been followers of Christ since they were children. Either way, we know that God is continually transforming us through his renewing Sprit, forming us into the glorious creation that he has always intended for us to be.

Prayer

Lord, you are renewing me day by day. Shape me into your masterpiece.

ABP

Change agents

[Christ Jesus] came and preached peace to you who were far away and peace to those who were near. For through him we both have access to the Father by one Spirit. Consequently, you are no longer foreigners and strangers, but fellow-citizens with God's people and also members of his household, built on the foundation of the apostles and prophets, with Christ Jesus himself as the chief cornerstone. In him the whole building is joined together and rises to become a holy temple in the Lord. And in him you too are being built together to become a dwelling in which God lives by his Spirit.

Over a decade ago I was transplanted to my husband's country, the UK. Suddenly, I felt helpless and disorientated. Even going to the post office was a trial, as I tried to remember the correct words or how much money the coins denoted. I was a foreigner and a stranger: I didn't belong. Then two women with experience of both countries befriended me, helping me to fit in. They were God's agents, preaching peace and helping me to look beyond my culture shock to God's greater purposes.

Paul in his letter also acts as an agent of change and peace. He moves from an emphasis on individual salvation to the divisions that had existed between Jewish believers and the new converts, the Gentiles. Whereas alienation once reigned, now Christ has smashed the dividing wall of hostility, ushering in unity and peace. Those who were warring with each other can now have enriching relationships.

Through Christ, we also have access to the Father through the Spirit and so we are citizens and members of his household. We are no longer foreigners or strangers, for now we belong to the household of God. We know that he welcomes us and will hear us.

Christ has dismantled the wall of division and also become the chief cornerstone of the building that is the people of God. Through him we too are part of this dwelling, interconnected and dependent on him and those around us. Let's ask ourselves this question: 'How can we be agents of peace this day?'

Prayer
Lord, we rejoice that you have not left us, but live in and through us.

ABP

Heirs together

In reading this, then, you will be able to understand my insight into the mystery of Christ, which was not made known to people in other generations... This mystery is that through the gospel the Gentiles are heirs together with Israel, members together of one body, and sharers together in the promise in Christ Jesus... Although I am less than the least of all the Lord's people, this grace was given me: to preach to the Gentiles the boundless riches of Christ, and to make plain to everyone the administration of this mystery, which for ages past was kept hidden in God, who created all things.

Years ago, I was visiting a pastor and his family and I remember my surprise when he remarked at how much he enjoyed his church council meetings. His voice was filled with delight as he marvelled over the creative ways God was using his body of believers. Too often, however, this is not the case. You can probably recall acrimonious church meetings as clearly as I can, when words are used as weapons and the character of people is called into question or even maligned. How God must weep at such divisions and strife.

Paul preaches God's peace and grace in his letter. He has moved from speaking of Christ's work of individual salvation and reconciliation to God's formation of the Church, which is for all, whatever our race. Paul stresses this aspect of unity with his repetition of the word 'together' (v. 6): Gentiles are heirs together with Israel and together they are members of one body; together they share in the promise of Christ.

That the Gentiles were deemed equal with their fellow Jewish believers must have been a surprise, for the newcomers would not have expected this level of equality. Through Christ, however, all divisions cease—Paul points the way to a new order. He makes known what was once hidden, administering the grace of God to the least in his kingdom.

Today, join me in praying for peace and unity among believers, that we will be God's sweet fragrance, inviting the world back to its Creator.

Reflection

'Just as a body, though one, has many parts, but all its many parts form one body, so it is with Christ' (1 Corinthians 12:12).

ABP

My heart, Christ's home

For this reason I kneel before the Father... I pray that out of his glorious riches he may strengthen you with power through his Spirit in your inner being, so that Christ may dwell in your hearts through faith. And I pray that you, being rooted and established in love, may have power, together with all the Lord's people, to grasp how wide and long and high and deep is the love of Christ, and to know this love that surpasses knowledge—that you may be filled to the measure of all the fullness of God.

This is one of the most inspiring passages of Paul's letter, showing how Christ takes residence in the believer, making his home in our inner being. It is trinitarian, for Paul prays that the Father would strengthen his children through his Spirit so that Christ may dwell in us. Christ lives in us and we live in Christ. He changes our outlook, attitudes and emotions, making us more like him. We then yearn for justice and mercy; we pray for those who wrong us; we can rest and be at peace.

Why and how? All through love. Through a love that is wide, long, high and deep, beyond our knowing. Some commentators dismiss these geographical descriptions as a mere poetical flourish, but I think they give a rich image of the all-surpassing vastness of God's love. John Stott tells of the ancient commentators who saw these dimensions illustrated on the cross of Christ: 'For its upright pole reached down into the earth and pointed up to heaven, while its crossbar carried the arms of Jesus, stretched out as if to invite and welcome the world' (*God's New Society*, IVP, p. 137). As he says, it may be fanciful, but it is true.

With Christ dwelling within, we are rooted and established in his love—rooted, as if a tree or a vine, and established, as if the foundation of a well-built building. Let us pray that this love permeates our lives today.

Prayer

'Now to him who is able to do immeasurably more than all we ask or imagine, according to his power that is at work within us, to him be glory in the church and in Christ Jesus throughout all generations, for ever and ever! Amen' (Ephesians 3:20–21).

ABP

23

The bond of peace

As a prisoner for the Lord, then, I urge you to live a life worthy of the calling you have received. Be completely humble and gentle; be patient, bearing with one another in love. Make every effort to keep the unity of the Spirit through the bond of peace. There is one body and one Spirit, just as you were called to one hope when you were called; one Lord, one faith, one baptism; one God and Father of all, who is over all and through all and in all.

Up until today's passage, Paul has not corrected or made demands on his readers. Then, in just a few lines, he lays out a series of directives for right living. Because Christ has made his home within us and we are rooted in his love, we are able to live in a way that brings glory to him. We can be humble, gentle and patient, put up with others in love and seek to keep unity.

Today, these attributes are counter-cultural. Humbleness can be seen as weakness, as an invitation for others to run riot over us. Gentleness can disappear like a vapour in the rough and tumble of life, as we rush from one important matter to the next. Patience wears thin when we have too many demands upon us and feel inadequate. Selfishness often supersedes loving each other and unity breaks down at the first whiff of conflict.

Yet, this is what we are called to and what we are equipped for with Christ at our centre. We were made for others and only experience the true riches of Christ when we live in community. Here we work out our faith, sometimes with fear and trembling. If we pause in the heat of the moment, reflecting that Christ lives within, we can apportion his grace to make us gentle and loving as we put our fellows before ourselves.

As you seek the one God and Father, the one Lord and the one Spirit, may you have hope and faith in him who is over, through and in all.

Reflection

'Do nothing out of selfish ambition or vain conceit. Rather, in humility value others above yourselves, not looking to your own interests but each of you to the interests of the others' (Philippians 2:3–4).

ABP

EPHESIANS 4:17–20, 22–24 (TNIV, ABRIDGED)

Old versus new

I tell you this, and insist on it in the Lord, that you must no longer live as the Gentiles do… They are darkened in their understanding and separated from the life of God because of the ignorance that is in them due to the hardening of their hearts. Having lost all sensitivity, they have given themselves over to sensuality so as to indulge in every kind of impurity, and they are full of greed. That, however, is not the way of life you learned… You were taught… to put off your old self, which is being corrupted by its deceitful desires; to be made new in the attitude of your minds; and to put on the new self, created to be like God in true righteousness and holiness.

When I started a job as a commissioning editor in London, I was overwhelmed by the many new things to learn. Some were obvious: colleagues' names, a different computer system, unfamiliar publications. Some, though, were below the surface, such as the working culture, personalities, expectations and emotions. I came home utterly exhausted, but, before long, my new editorial life felt comfortable and familiar.

Here, Paul urges his readers to leave their old lives of sin behind. Though the new converts were still living next to the Gentiles, they were not to mimic their actions or their hardness of heart. Instead, they were to put on their new selves, which would reflect God's holiness. Paul speaks of the old and new selves throughout his letters. For example: 'Our old self was crucified with him' (Romans 6:6); 'Do not lie to each other, since you have taken off your old self' (Colossians 3:9); 'Clothe yourselves with the Lord Jesus Christ' (Romans 13:14). Employing this baptismal language, he yearns for the new believers to commit themselves fully to the ways of Christ, leaving greed and impurity behind.

What do we need to leave behind from our old selves? A not-too-edifying TV drama? A spirit of complaining? A lack of thankfulness? Join me in asking the Lord to illuminate those areas where we are corrupted, that our minds and hearts may be renewed.

Prayer
Lord, we want to be made clean and holy. Help us to embrace the new life you are forming in us.

ABP

EPHESIANS 4:25–32 (TNIV, ABRIDGED)

How to live

Therefore each of you must put off falsehood and speak truthfully to your neighbour… 'In your anger do not sin': do not let the sun go down while you are still angry, and do not give the devil a foothold. Those who have been stealing must steal no longer, but must work, doing something useful with their own hands… Do not let any unwholesome talk come out of your mouths, but only what is helpful for building others up… And do not grieve the Holy Spirit of God, with whom you were sealed for the day of redemption. Get rid of all bitterness, rage and anger, brawling and slander, along with every form of malice. Be kind and compassionate to one another, forgiving each other, just as in Christ God forgave you.

After exploring theological concepts—such as how we live in Christ—Paul turns to a practical set of instructions as he continues teaching on the old versus the new. Each of these commands, as John Stott says in *God's New Society*, addresses our relationships. Holiness does not occur in a vacuum, but in the real world that we inhabit with those around us.

Stott also shows how each of the commands starts off with a negative prohibition, followed by a positive action. For example, do not lie, but speak the truth to your neighbour. Have righteous anger, but don't nurse your anger. Stop stealing; make your hands useful by working. Don't speak unkindly, but build others up with your words. Don't grieve the Holy Spirit, for you are sealed with him. Eradicate any bitterness, rage, fighting and malice; instead be kind and filled with compassion as you forgive each other.

Old habits can die hard, though; we need God's grace and help to change our ways. Today, why not take Paul's list and ask God to help you 'change one thing' (in the words of a recent high-street campaign). Instead of tearing down your spouse or friend, pay them a compliment. Ask the Lord to give you compassion for someone who annoys you.

May God help us live out of our new selves as we put off the old.

Prayer
Lord, sometimes I speak before I think about what I'm saying. Reign over my tongue, that I might bring glory to you.

ABP

EPHESIANS 5:3–5, 8–10 (TNIV)

How much is enough?

But among you there must not be even a hint of sexual immorality, or of any kind of impurity, or of greed, because these are improper for the Lord's people. Nor should there be obscenity, foolish talk or coarse joking, which are out of place, but rather thanksgiving. For of this you can be sure: no immoral, impure or greedy person— such a person is an idolater—has any inheritance in the kingdom of Christ and of God... For you were once darkness, but now you are light in the Lord. Live as children of light (for the fruit of the light consists in all goodness, righteousness and truth) and find out what pleases the Lord.

Leo Tolstoy posed an age-old question in the title of his 1886 short story, *How Much Land Does a Man Need?* His main character has been bitten by the land bug, so, once he completes one purchase, he seeks out the next deal. Then, one day he is given a chance to stake out as much land as he can cover by foot, as long as he returns to the starting point by sundown. He greedily runs farther and farther, only turning back when he realises that the sun is setting. He makes it back to the starting point just in time, but drops dead from exhaustion. How much land does a man need? Just six feet—enough for a grave.

Paul knows that greed, when left unchecked, can grow and flourish like a weed. He wants to stamp out even hints of it, along with other sins, such as sexual immorality and obscenity. Sexual sin was rife in biblical times, including prostitution, sexual misuse of slaves and promiscuity. Our culture, too, remains sex-craved and sex-saturated. No one is immune—impurity can enter our minds and bodies like a worm, growing ever stronger as it feeds on our desires.

No longer can we dwell in that darkness; now we are actually light in the Lord. Light dispels darkness, so as we live before, in and through Christ, we will glow in his holy light and bear the fruit Paul mentions— namely, goodness, righteousness and truth. Let us seek to be content with his riches, not desiring more than he has chosen to bequeath to us.

Prayer
Lord, give me peace in your presence and help me to be content.

ABP

Filled with the Spirit

Be very careful, then, how you live—not as unwise but as wise, making the most of every opportunity, because the days are evil. Therefore do not be foolish, but understand what the Lord's will is. Do not get drunk on wine... Instead, be filled with the Spirit, speaking to one another with psalms, hymns and songs from the Spirit. Sing and make music from your heart to the Lord, always giving thanks to God the Father for everything, in the name of our Lord Jesus Christ. Submit to one another out of reverence for Christ.

Many modern translations of today's passage start a new section at verse 21 ('Submit to one another...') instead of having verses 18–21 as one sentence, as they are in the Greek (starting with 'Do not get drunk...'). When we understand how the text fits together, writes Klyne Snodgrass in *The NIV Application Commentary*, we see that Paul is telling his readers five ways to be filled by the Spirit: speak to one another with psalms, sing, make music, give thanks, submit to one another out of reverence for Christ.

Why does this matter? Because, as Snodgrass says, 'Failure to understand the structure has made this section one of the most misappropriated texts in the Bible' (p. 286). The 'house codes' that follow, about how wives and husbands, children and parents, slaves and masters should treat each other, all fall under the command of mutual submission under Christ. Because we live in holy fear of God, we submit to each other. This entails humility, sacrificial love and putting others above ourselves.

As we cast away our old selves and put on the new, we start to live a life controlled not by wine but by the Spirit. The careful living that Paul describes entails the filling of the Holy Spirit, empowering us to act in a holy way that is pleasing to God. Through his Spirit we can sing, make music, give thanks—and submit to others.

Reflection

'In your relationships with one another, have the same attitude of mind Christ Jesus had: who... made himself nothing by taking the very nature of a servant, being made in human likeness' (Philippians 2:5–7).

ABP

EPHESIANS 6:10–13 (TNIV)

The unseen real

Finally, be strong in the Lord and in his mighty power. Put on the full armour of God, so that you can take your stand against the devil's schemes. For our struggle is not against flesh and blood, but against the rulers, against the authorities, against the powers of this dark world and against the spiritual forces of evil in the heavenly realms. Therefore put on the full armour of God, so that when the day of evil comes, you may be able to stand your ground, and after you have done everything, to stand.

As a book editor, I meet fascinating people. One is a woman who was once entrenched in the occult. Through it she was nearly destroyed, but she came to a saving faith in Jesus hours before she was planning to commit suicide. In doing so and afterwards, however, she endured a spiritual battle on a scale and level that most of us will be spared (Lulu Auger, *Lulu*, Chosen Books, 2009.)

If we follow Christ, we will all engage in spiritual battle. God allows Satan to operate on earth and this fallen creature is utterly opposed to the redeeming work of Christ. As collaborators with Christ, though, we can stand our ground through God's power and send Satan away.

Many people today don't believe that the devil or demons exist. Some Christians fall prey to this materialist belief, contrary to Paul's letter. Of course, others hold a view at the opposite extreme, seeing the devil everywhere and ascribing to him every fallen action or occurrence. Here, though, as Paul draws his letter to a close, he simply wants his recipients to open their eyes to the unseen world and prepare for action.

He reveals the cosmic nature of the battle—we are fighting the rulers, powers and spiritual forces of evil in the heavenly realms. We know that the battle between God and the evil one is not equal, for Satan will be vanquished, and we need not fear.

Reflection

There are two equal and opposite errors into which our race can fall about the devils. One is to disbelieve in their existence. The other is to believe, and to feel an excessive and unhealthy interest in them.

C.S. Lewis, *The Screwtape Letters* (1942)

ABP

The armour of God

Stand firm then, with the belt of truth buckled round your waist, with the breastplate of righteousness in place, and with your feet fitted with the readiness that comes from the gospel of peace. In addition to all this, take up the shield of faith, with which you can extinguish all the flaming arrows of the evil one. Take the helmet of salvation and the sword of the Spirit, which is the word of God. And pray in the Spirit on all occasions with all kinds of prayers and requests. With this in mind, be alert and always keep on praying for all the Lord's people.

Paul was writing his letter to the Ephesians while in chains, so a Roman soldier may have been standing next to him, decked out in full armour. Paul employed this military imagery and also drew on the language of battles in the Old Testament, in particular Isaiah. For example, in Isaiah 11:5, the Messiah has righteousness as his belt and faithfulness as the sash round his waist. Righteousness is also his breastplate in 59:17, along with the helmet of salvation. And the 'feet fitted with the readiness' hearken back to 52:7: 'How beautiful on the mountains are the feet of those who bring good news'.

Paul's use of this imagery is much more memorable than if he had said, 'Stand firm with truth, righteousness, faith, salvation, the word of God and prayer.' Indeed, I know of one minister who, before she goes into a potentially difficult meeting, prepares by putting on each piece of armour—complete with the physical motions. By doing so she reclaims the Lord's resources that she needs to stand against any evil forces while she seeks to usher in the gospel of peace and righteousness.

Paul's instructions, as with his whole letter, are not just for individual believers but for us as a community. We are strengthened as we stand together, holding our shields of faith against the flaming arrows of the evil one. While doing so, we pray for ourselves and for all the Lord's people, that we might stand firm in him.

Prayer

Lord, thank you for this journey through Paul's letter to the Ephesians.
May your truth permeate our beings, that we might bring you glory.

ABP

Strangely warmed: the Wesleyan revival

This week many churches celebrate John and Charles Wesley, the brothers who, in the 18th century, with George Whitefield, changed the face of Christianity in the British Isles. For the next fortnight, following on from Pentecost, we shall be looking at how the Holy Spirit spoke to them through the scriptures, reawakening their faith, and how the Spirit can speak to us with the same effect today.

John and Charles were the sons of a parson. Both went to Oxford University and were ordained in the Church of England. At Oxford they formed a religious society called the Holy Club, and were dubbed 'the Methodists' by their fellow students because they were so 'methodical' in their Christian discipline. The name stuck and became the name of the movement that arose from their preaching.

After a disappointing time as a missionary in America, John Wesley returned to England, feeling that there was a missing element of authenticity in his faith. Joining up with the Moravians in London, he was impressed by the depth of their trust in Christ. It was at a Moravian meeting in 1738, while listening to a reading of Luther's preface to the epistle to the Romans, that he famously felt his heart 'strangely warmed' and did 'trust Christ, and Christ alone' for his salvation. Charles had a similar experience the following year.

John became an itinerant preacher—largely because the pulpits of most churches were barred to him. Charles was more of a traditionalist, but from time to time joined John in his nationwide ministry. Huge crowds flocked to hear the message and groups of people who were touched by it began to gather together to pray and praise. Their praise was wonderfully enhanced by the hymns written by Charles, one of the best and most prolific hymn writers of the Christian Church.

There were three long-term consequences of the Wesleys' ministry. First, a moribund church and largely godless society were awakened to the challenge of the gospel. Second, a new force emerged in Christendom—the Methodist Church. Third, the evangelical movement in the Church of England brought fresh life and vitality to not only many parishes but also the life of the nation, through men like Wilberforce and Shaftesbury, and to the world, through its missionaries.

David Winter

ACTS 2:14–18, 20–21 (NRSV, ABRIDGED)

A new thing

But Peter... addressed them: 'Men of Judea and all who live in Jerusalem, let this be known to you, and listen to what I say. Indeed, these are not drunk, as you suppose, for it is only nine o'clock in the morning. No, this is what was spoken through the prophet Joel: "In the last days it will be, God declares, that I will pour out my Spirit upon all flesh, and your sons and your daughters shall prophesy, and your young men shall see visions, and your old men shall dream dreams. Even upon my slaves, both men and women, in those days I will pour out my Spirit; and they shall prophesy... The sun shall be turned to darkness and the moon to blood, before the coming of the Lord's great and glorious day. Then everyone who calls on the name of the Lord shall be saved."'

This is part of Peter's speech to the crowds on the day of Pentecost, 50 days after Jesus' crucifixion and resurrection. The first thing the people on the streets knew of the event was when the disciples emerged from the upper room (vv. 1–2), speaking in many different languages. So astonishing was the sight, some bystanders thought that they must be drunk, presumably because to many of them their speech sounded like gibberish. No, Peter assured them, these people are not drunk. On the contrary, a centuries-old prophecy was being fulfilled—the pouring out of God's Spirit not just on chosen individuals but also on 'all flesh' (Jews and Gentiles, men and women, young and old). This was a completely new thing, a work of the Creator Spirit, no less.

This Pentecostal effect has been seen in the history of the Church in many historic 'revivals'—times when the Church has been renewed, its message refreshed and its members transformed by the work of the Spirit. In Luke's account, Peter sees in this a foretaste of the promised 'Day of the Lord', at the climax of history, but it is also and more immediately a reminder that the same Spirit is constantly at work in the Church—and in the world.

Reflection

Whenever we speak out the word of God, dream dreams and see visions of his blessing, God's Spirit is at work among us.

DW

Grace, through faith

But God, who is rich in mercy, out of the great love with which he loved us even when we were dead through our trespasses, made us alive together with Christ—by grace you have been saved—and raised us up with him and seated us with him in the heavenly places in Christ Jesus, so that in the ages to come he might show the immeasurable riches of his grace in kindness towards us in Christ Jesus. For by grace you have been saved through faith, and this is not your own doing; it is the gift of God—not the result of works, so that no one may boast. For we are what he has made us, created in Christ Jesus for good works, which God prepared beforehand to be our way of life.

This passage pretty well sums up the message of the Wesleyan Revival, bringing together two key elements of the Wesley brothers' theology: justification by grace through faith and, flowing from that, a life of holiness and loving service—the 'good works' God intends to be the hallmark of the Christian life. The message was not, strictly speaking, 'new' at all. One can trace it from Paul's letter to the Romans in the first century through to the teaching of Augustine of Hippo in the fifth and then to the Augustinian monk Martin Luther in the 16th. Indeed, grace had always been given priority in Christian theology, but, at different periods, it had got overlaid with rules, ceremonies and the constant human desire to justify ourselves. Justification by grace through faith can only be received in humble trust. Those who think they can save themselves will always be reluctant to let Christ do it for them!

The recurrent phrase here is 'in Christ Jesus'. Three times the apostle stresses that all of these blessings are 'in Christ [the Messiah] Jesus'. Paul, too, uses this phrase endlessly in his letters, with two slightly different meanings. 'In Christ' means to be a member of his Body, the Church. It also describes the standing of the individual Christian, who is 'in Christ'—that is, held within his saving love and grace.

Reflection

To trust Christ, 'and Christ alone', for salvation was the conversion experience of John Wesley. It is the heart of Paul's message, too.

DW

The voices that could not be silenced

Now when [the religious authorities] saw the boldness of Peter and John and realised that they were uneducated and ordinary men, they were amazed and recognised them as companions of Jesus. When they saw the man who had been cured standing beside them, they had nothing to say in opposition. So they ordered them to leave the council while they discussed the matter with one another. They said, 'What will we do with them? For it is obvious to all who live in Jerusalem that a notable sign has been done through them... But to keep it from spreading further among the people, let us warn them to speak no more to anyone in this name.' So they... ordered them not to speak or teach at all in the name of Jesus. But Peter and John answered them, 'Whether it is right in God's sight to listen to you rather than to God, you must judge; for we cannot keep from speaking about what we have seen and heard.'

After Pentecost, the apostles were full of enthusiasm to share the good news about Jesus. When, as in the case of the lame man healed by Peter and John (3:1–10), their words were accompanied by miraculous signs, it was hard for the 'powers that be' to ignore them. So the two apostles were arrested and brought before the religious authorities. How could the authorities contain this potentially dangerous teaching—dangerous, that is, to the delicate balance between the Roman occupiers and the temple hierarchy, and to their own position and prestige?

Their answer was to give Peter and John what we would call an 'official warning'. 'Don't do it again', they said. They were probably surprised at the apostles' response. Far from promising to keep quiet, they pointed out that, as their message was God's, they could not possibly keep quiet about it. The Wesleys and Whitefield in the 18th century took the same position. No authority, secular or religious, could forbid them to share what they were convinced was gospel truth. It cost the Wesleys some prestigious pulpits and ecclesiastical honours, but it brought blessings to tens of thousands of ordinary people.

Reflection

'We cannot keep quiet'—not when a matter of eternal life is at stake.

DW

Fighting against God

When [the high priest and the council] heard [the words of Peter and the apostles], they were enraged and wanted to kill them. But a Pharisee in the council named Gamaliel, a teacher of the law, respected by all the people, stood up and ordered the men to be put outside for a short time. Then he said to them, 'Fellow Israelites, consider carefully what you propose to do to these men... I tell you, keep away from these men and let them alone; because if this plan or this undertaking is of human origin, it will fail; but if it is of God, you will not be able to overthrow them—in that case you may even be found fighting against God!' They were convinced by him.

The religious revival headed by John Wesley and George Whitefield provoked a similar response from the Church authorities as the apostles' preaching did after Pentecost. The terrible religious conflicts of the previous century made people wary of views that seemed to inflame passion or stir up disorder. One bishop warned Wesley, 'Enthusiasm is a dreadful thing, Mr Wesley—a very dreadful thing indeed!' As in apostolic times, however, there were those who could distinguish between empty enthusiasm and a genuine work of God and gradually this renewal was accepted as something not to be deplored but welcomed. While this was happening, though, many pulpits were barred to Wesley's preachers and many clergy who followed his lead were ostracised.

Gamaliel emerges here as one of the genuinely wise men of his day. He was a Pharisee, like Saul of Tarsus, but he was also a man of true spiritual insight. His argument carried the day with the council. If this movement was purely human, it would fail, but if it was of God they could do nothing to stop it. Why, he warned them, we—the religious leaders of Israel—might be found to be 'fighting against God'. It is encouraging to read in the New Testament of several such men—Joseph of Arimathea, Nicodemus, Gamaliel—who held truth and justice to be greater than political expediency.

Reflection

If we fear that the gospel's momentum has been lost, we need to remember Gamaliel's words. 'If this is of God, then nothing and nobody can stop it.'

DW

For the sake of the name

They were convinced by [Gamaliel], and when they had called in the apostles, they had them flogged. Then they ordered them not to speak in the name of Jesus, and let them go. As they left the council, they rejoiced that they were considered worthy to suffer dishonour for the sake of the name. And every day in the temple and at home they did not cease to teach and proclaim Jesus as the Messiah.

It sounds like rough justice: agreeing with Gamaliel's advice to 'let these men alone', the religious authorities 'had them flogged'! If that was intended to deter them from their preaching, though, it was a lost cause. Remembering the words of Jesus—'Blessed are you when people revile you and persecute you' (Matthew 5:11)—they 'rejoiced' in their suffering (v. 41) and simply went on proclaiming their message. It was 'for the sake of the name'—the 'name above every name' that Paul speaks of, the name at which one day 'every knee should bend, in heaven and on earth and under the earth' (Philippians 2:10), which is the name of Jesus, the Messiah and Lord. He was their higher authority, the one who commanded their total obedience and loyalty.

Seventeen centuries later, the preachers of the Wesleyan revival suffered similar opposition. At times they were cursed, at times missiles were thrown at them, at times they were physically assaulted. Nothing deterred them. Like the apostles, they 'rejoiced' that they too were considered worthy to suffer 'for the sake of the name'. This determination undoubtedly played a part in winning over public support. The more the opposition clamoured, the larger grew the crowds wanting to hear John Wesley and his companions. The movement was 'of God', so human opposition, no matter how bitter or powerful, was useless. The result was exactly the same as it was back in the time of the apostles: 'during those days... the disciples were increasing in number' (Acts 6:1).

Reflection

Opposition and persecution are never to be deliberately sought, but when they are the response to faithful witness and a Christian lifestyle, they have often proved to be the Church's most effective tool for evangelism.

DW

ROMANS 5:1–5 (NRSV)

The possibility of holy living

Therefore, since we are justified by faith, we have peace with God through our Lord Jesus Christ, through whom we have obtained access to this grace in which we stand; and we boast in our hope of sharing the glory of God. And not only that, but we also boast in our sufferings, knowing that suffering produces endurance, and endurance produces character, and character produces hope, and hope does not disappoint us, because God's love has been poured into our hearts through the Holy Spirit that has been given to us.

I said on Monday that there were two elements to the Wesleyan message: justification by grace through faith and, flowing from that, a life of holiness and loving service. At this point in Paul's letter, he has more or less completed his powerful advocacy of the principle of justification: the sinner is counted as righteous not because of personal reformation of life, but inward conversion of spirit ('grace').

Now he moves on to the consequences. 'Having been justified by faith' (the tense is past passive: it has already happened to us), we have 'peace with God', true *shalom*, total well-being, a unity of purpose. Then follows an escalating list of developments. We have 'access' to God's grace: there are no barriers or intermediaries between us and blessing. We discover that suffering has a purpose, because it can create endurance. This is more than simply a capacity to 'put up with it'. Rather, it sees suffering, accepted in the right spirit, as helping to develop 'character'. All around us are people for whom the experience of suffering has not led to bitterness or despair, but to the growth of faith and hope. 'Hope' of that kind is the final blessing of justification because, through it, God's love is poured into our hearts through the Holy Spirit. Here is a wonderful picture of divine generosity: the love of God is emptied into our hearts like a jug of fresh water!

Reflection

Using passages like this, the Wesleys built their emphasis on the possibility of a life of God-given holiness. You can find it in phrases from Charles' hymns, such as 'Finish then thy new creation, pure and spotless let us be' (from 'Love divine, all loves excelling', 1747).

DW

1 CORINTHIANS 9:16–18 (NRSV)

Required to preach

If I proclaim the gospel, this gives me no ground for boasting, for an obligation is laid on me, and woe betide me if I do not proclaim the gospel! For if I do this of my own will, I have a reward; but if not of my own will, I am entrusted with a commission. What then is my reward? Just this: that in my proclamation I may make the gospel free of charge, so as not to make full use of my rights in the gospel.

The Wesley brothers would have said that every Christian had a responsibility to be a witness to Christ. At the same time, they recognised a distinct ministry of preaching, by both lay and ordained people. Local (lay) preachers were—and still are—essential elements in the growth of the Methodist Church and, indeed, of most other denominations. John Wesley broke the recognised pattern of ministry at the time because, although an ordained Anglican minister, he preached wherever he felt the Spirit led him—in the open air (a scandal at the time) and without regard to parish boundaries. He saw his ministry as being like the apostle Paul's. He shared the same inner compulsion to preach and his 'commission' came from the highest possible authority—Jesus Christ himself. He needed neither a licence to preach nor a stipend to support him (though Paul argued strongly that others were entitled to be paid for their ministry). In this way, both men sought to remove any allegations that they were lining their own pockets through their ministry.

Charles never entirely shared this freelance view of Christian ministry, but, between John and his brother and with the support of a growing band of preachers, they carried the message to the ends of the British Isles and far beyond. The Wesleys recognised that there were many men—and women—who lacked the theological education that they had had, but were nevertheless called to preach. 'How can they hear without a preacher?' Paul asked elsewhere (Romans 10:14). This great company of preachers was the Wesleys' answer to his question!

Reflection

All are called to bear witness, some are called to preach, all are called to pray that the 'Lord of the harvest' will 'send labourers out into his harvest' (Matthew 9:38) and some are called to go and do it!

DW

1 Corinthians 9:19–23 (NRSV)

All things to all people

For though I am free with respect to all, I have made myself a slave to all, so that I might win more of them. To the Jews I became as a Jew, in order to win Jews. To those under the law I became as one under the law (though I myself am not under the law) so that I might win those under the law. To those outside the law I became as one outside the law (though I am not free from God's law but am under Christ's law) so that I might win those outside the law. To the weak I became weak, so that I might win the weak. I have become all things to all people, so that I might by any means save some. I do it all for the sake of the gospel, so that I may share in its blessings.

'Oh,' I've heard people say, 'I don't trust him. He's all things to all men.' Well, the words might be Paul's, but the meaning is exactly the opposite of his. For him, the key to Christian witness and ministry was to identify as completely as possible with the people to whom he wished to witness or preach, to enter into their thinking, see things through their eyes, not in order to ingratiate himself with them, but to win them for Christ.

As a matter of textual fact, he didn't say 'men', either, though that is how the phrase has entered our language. He used the word for 'everyone'. Paul's appeal was to the whole human race—Jews, Gentiles, slaves, the powerful and the weak, men and women. Whether they were deeply religious Jews or secular Greeks, powerful leaders or powerless slaves, his message was essentially the same: he proclaimed 'Christ crucified' (1:23). The mind that framed the message and the voice that spoke it were tuned to the particular needs and circumstances of those who heard it, but what was true in the first century was equally true in the 18th and is now in the 21st. The gospel is alive and living things adapt in order to survive and grow.

Reflection

This is the opposite of a ghetto Christianity, which demands that people come to us, accept our ways and adopt our culture if they are to share 'our' good news.

DW

ROMANS 8:14–17 (NRSV)

Joint heirs with Christ

For all who are led by the Spirit of God are children of God. For
you did not receive a spirit of slavery to fall back into fear, but you
have received a spirit of adoption. When we cry, 'Abba! Father!'
it is that very Spirit bearing witness with our spirit that we are
children of God, and if children, then heirs, heirs of God and joint
heirs with Christ—if, in fact, we suffer with him so that we may
also be glorified with him.

In Christian history, movements of revival, like the Wesleyan Revival
250 years ago, liberate ordinary people from the limitations of their
daily life. Through their newfound faith they experience a fresh dignity
and sense of purpose. Often uneducated people have become great
leaders of the Church—rather like the first apostles of Christ, most
of whom were fishermen or Galilean country folk. Paul describes this
process in terms of adoption into a new and glorious family, the family
of 'the children of God'. This phrase is often used to describe all human
beings, simply because they are his creatures, but Paul has a nobler
image in mind. Formerly we were 'slaves' of fear, but, through faith in
Jesus, the Spirit of God has given us a new standing. We are 'adopted'
members of God's family, with all the privileges that go with it.

As his adopted children, we are truly God's sons and daughters in
the fullest sense. The language is extravagant, daring even. We are God's
'heirs'. His inheritance is ours. His riches are ours. His heavenly home
is ours. In case there is any doubt about his meaning, Paul carries this
to its logical conclusion: if we are 'heirs of God', then we are 'joint
heirs' with Christ. Christians share in his cross ('I have been crucified
with Christ', Galatians 2:19) and they also share in his glory. It's hard
to think of a greater destiny than sharing Christ's glory. No wonder
the converted farm labourer and the weary mother washing the family
clothes in the village river felt a new dignity and sense of worth.

Reflection

*Christian conversion often sets people free to fulfil undreamt-of possibilities
in their lives. The Methodist movement tapped a rich vein of lay ministry
and service. The adopted children revelled in their new sense of worth!*

DW

The mind of the Spirit

For in hope we were saved. Now hope that is seen is not hope. For who hopes for what is seen? But if we hope for what we do not see, we wait for it with patience. Likewise the Spirit helps us in our weakness; for we do not know how to pray as we ought, but that very Spirit intercedes with sighs too deep for words. And God, who searches the heart, knows what is the mind of the Spirit, because the Spirit intercedes for the saints according to the will of God.

Often one of the most obvious results of renewal in the Church is in the area of prayer. It is easy for prayer to become a rather tired routine— something we do without any sense that we are about vital spiritual business. Then, with a fresh awareness of the Holy Spirit's reality, what had been tired and routine becomes dynamic and life-changing. It's a bit like rewiring an old house where the electricity had supposedly been switched off long ago, but suddenly getting an electric shock! Such a renewal of prayer was a major consequence of the Wesleyan Revival. Churches and Christians whose prayer had become formal and dead found new life. People prayed spontaneously, those who turned to the liturgy found that it came alive and some who had never felt able to pray were liberated to do so.

In this passage, Paul goes to the heart of the matter. We pray to the Father in the power of the Spirit and in union with Christ and, when we can't find words or our emotions are so overwhelming that words cannot express them, the Spirit takes over, praying for us 'with sighs too deep for words'. The Spirit prompts and guides our prayers, though the lips that utter them are ours. The Spirit also interprets our words to the Father, 'intercedes' for us—places himself between us and God as a means of communication. In that way, we can be sure that our prayers are in line with the will of God.

Reflection

The power of a laser lies in the fact that oscillations which might
otherwise cancel each other out operate in harmony. Such 'harmony'
is also the power of prayer—God's will and mine perfectly in tune,
harmonised by the Holy Spirit.

DW

More than conquerors

Who will separate us from the love of Christ? Will hardship, or distress, or persecution, or famine, or nakedness, or peril, or sword? As it is written, 'For your sake we are being killed all day long; we are accounted as sheep to be slaughtered.' No, in all these things we are more than conquerors through him who loved us. For I am convinced that neither death, nor life, nor angels, nor rulers, nor things present, nor things to come, nor powers, nor height, nor depth, nor anything else in all creation, will be able to separate us from the love of God in Christ Jesus our Lord.

Most people don't associate Paul with poetic language but, in fact, from time to time his rather pedestrian Greek takes off and sings. We recognise it in his famous hymn to love (1 Corinthians 13), but I think this glorious passage tops them all.

Let's remember that Paul was writing to a group of Christians living in the heart of the great Roman Empire, on the very doorstep of the Emperor himself. Already there were signs that the authorities were getting impatient with these wretched Christians, whose very presence seemed to provoke civil unrest. Some of those listening to his words would have been slaves whose lives were often bleak and hopeless. Some would have been minor officials and employees of the State who might have feared for their futures if and when their Christian faith was revealed. All lived in a society where rigid social demarcations meant that some groups of people were permanently separated from others.

Yet here, the apostle draws a picture of a new society, one in which nothing—just look how the word 'nothing' is underlined and emphasised with example after example—can separate the believer from the love of God. Paul is convinced, and wants to convince them, that 'nothing', not even death itself, nor any human or supernatural power, can drive a wedge between them and their standing in Christ before God.

Reflection

This passage is often read at the start of funeral services and, indeed, it does offer the ultimate assurance that those who die 'in Christ' are secure in the love of God 'through Christ Jesus our Lord.'

DW

The new community

For as in one body we have many members, and not all the members have the same function, so we, who are many, are one body in Christ, and individually we are members one of another. We have gifts that differ according to the grace given to us: prophecy, in proportion to faith; ministry, in ministering; the teacher, in teaching; the exhorter, in exhortation; the giver, in generosity; the leader, in diligence; the compassionate, in cheerfulness. Let love be genuine; hate what is evil; hold fast to what is good; love one another with mutual affection; outdo one another in showing honour. Do not lag in zeal, be ardent in spirit, serve the Lord. Rejoice in hope, be patient in suffering, persevere in prayer. Contribute to the needs of the saints; extend hospitality to strangers.

The 'body' in the first sentence is, of course, the human body and the 'members' are its limbs and organs. We need fingers, but they can't do the seeing for us. Ears are useful, but so are feet. Each 'member' has a role to fulfil—some are more obviously 'important', but, in practice, we need them all. It's but a small step from this image to Paul's picture of the 'body' of the church—here, we assume, the local church, which is a part of the great Body of Christ on earth and in heaven.

In our local churches, we need to recognise that each member has a distinctive role to play if the whole body is to function properly. The recovery of that truth has been at the heart of every revival in the Church. Not all of us have highly visible roles, but we each have vital contributions to make. Some are generous givers, some work diligently at whatever task they're given, some care for the sick and sorrowing and some have a ministry of cheerfulness (every church can do with that!). There is no hierarchy to these gifts, they are simply different, and the difference, we need to keep remembering, is 'according to the grace given to us'. The giver is the Holy Spirit.

Reflection

This passage turns the theory of spiritual gifting into practical application. This is what a church can be like if each member responds to their calling: hospitable, loving, compassionate, generous, prayerful and hopeful.

DW

Friday 4 June

EPHESIANS 6:13–17 (NRSV)

The armour of God

Therefore take up the whole armour of God, so that you may be able to withstand on that evil day, and having done everything, to stand firm. Stand therefore, and fasten the belt of truth around your waist, and put on the breastplate of righteousness. As shoes for your feet put on whatever will make you ready to proclaim the gospel of peace. With all of these, take the shield of faith, with which you will be able to quench all the flaming arrows of the evil one. Take the helmet of salvation, and the sword of the Spirit, which is the word of God.

The fact that Charles Wesley took this passage as the basis of one of his most popular hymns ('Soldiers of Christ, Arise!') shows how central its message is to Christian discipleship. The Wesleys were concerned from the very beginning of the spiritual renewal that flowed from their ministry that it should have depth as well as breadth. The commission of Christ was not to make 'converts' but disciples.

Consequently, they wanted those affected by the revival not to simply join new groups but also to embrace a whole way of life that involved personal discipline as the root of discipleship. The apostle sets out in this well-known passage the building blocks of such a disciplined life. It begins with *truth*—the apostolic message about Jesus, crucified and risen. It requires *righteousness*—doing what God requires. It is based on the gospel of *peace*—the good news that Jesus has made 'peace through the blood of his cross' (Colossians 1:20). It is sustained by faith, which, like a shield in battle, protects us from the arrows of doubt or despair. Its purpose is salvation, wholeness of body, mind and spirit—being what God intends us to be.

These are all 'defensive' weapons. The Christian is permitted one 'offensive' weapon: the 'sword of the Spirit'—'the word of God'. The Greek word is *rhema*, which means an actual spoken word: we could translate it as 'whatever God says'. That is what we have to offer—not our wisdom, or even our faith, but the word of the God who speaks.

Reflection

Armour is not much use left in the armoury. 'Put it on!' says the apostle.

DW

44

Sing with gratitude

Above all, clothe yourselves with love, which binds everything together in perfect harmony. And let the peace of Christ rule in your hearts, to which indeed you were called in the one body. And be thankful. Let the word of Christ dwell in you richly; teach and admonish one another in all wisdom; and with gratitude in your hearts sing psalms, hymns, and spiritual songs to God. And whatever you do, in word or deed, do everything in the name of the Lord Jesus, giving thanks to God the Father through him.

This passage could almost be a description of the early Methodist 'class meeting'. John Wesley was concerned that those touched by the revival should be nurtured rather than left to the mercy of the rather formal religion that dominated most of the churches of his time. Perhaps with this kind of Bible passage in mind, he devised a system of informal groups. Each had a leader but, above all, they were places where the Bible could be taught and studied. Questions could be asked and participants would be encouraged—and occasionally rebuked! Not only does the Methodist Church still operate such groups but almost every other Christian tradition incorporates similar gatherings, whether they are called 'cell' groups, home meetings or post-Alpha or Emmaus courses.

The picture Paul draws is very attractive. We can imagine the scene—perhaps a Sunday evening in Colossae, with a group of Christians meeting in someone's house. The group might include a wealthy merchant and his wife, a shopkeeper, widow or widower, one or two servants and slaves, maybe a church deacon or deaconess. They would perhaps recite a story of Jesus or part of the Sermon on the Mount together, then discuss it. They would share their experiences of the past week, asking for prayer and offering it for others. Also, of course, they would sing (that would appeal to Charles!) psalms, hymns and 'spiritual songs'. My guess is that such meetings probably lasted long into the night.

Reflection

Christian faith works best when it is rooted in the soil of a living fellowship.

DW

Mentoring

'Mentoring' is a term that is used to describe the process by which one person enables another to grow and develop. It is used widely in education and business as well as within the Church. In the Christian context, it is often known as *spiritual* mentoring because the purpose is to help individuals reach their full potential in God.

Most mentoring happens informally, as what we might call 'soul friendship'. Here, we encourage each other in our walk with God in the course of daily life—over a cup of coffee, as we walk and talk together or as we chat after a church service. Most of us will have had friends who came alongside us at crucial moments on our Christian journey, teaching or sharing with us from their own experience, and occasionally helping us discover God's will. They probably would never have thought of themselves as 'mentors', but mentoring is what they were doing.

Increasingly, people are seeing the benefits of a more intentional approach to mentoring. This is not something new, of course, and spiritual direction (to give it another name) has been around for a long time. We can all benefit from the wise counsel of those who are ahead of us on the journey and processing our thoughts and feelings in the presence of someone who will listen to us with understanding and discernment.

In some churches, mentoring is already well established as an effective way of discipling new believers and establishing them in the faith. Perhaps its greatest benefit, however, is in helping mature believers continue to make progress in their relationship with God. Generally speaking, while a local church may be good at getting people started on the Christian pathway, it may not be as good at enabling the onward journey of those individuals into a deeper and richer experience of God. Furthermore, it can be common for seasoned believers to become stalled as they walk the path of faith. Doubts can arise and cherished beliefs can start to seem less certain. Life experience can challenge our understanding of God's ways. Where can we go with our questions? Who will listen to us as we explore the issues? A trusted mentor can provide a safe haven for us to consider what is happening and help us navigate our way across the stormy seas.

Tony Horsfall

The philosophy behind mentoring

Blessed are those whose strength is in you, who have set their hearts on pilgrimage. As they pass through the Valley of Baca, they make it a place of springs; the autumn rains also cover it with pools. They go from strength to strength, till each appears before God in Zion.

Psalm 84 was one of the songs often sung by those on their way to Jerusalem to worship God. Three times a year the people were required to make such a pilgrimage and, while some probably did so reluctantly, for the writer of this psalm it was a joyous occasion.

Spiritual mentoring is built on the metaphor of the journey and here we are reminded that we are pilgrims who share a sacred journey together. It is always safer, and more enjoyable, to travel with others and the idea of 'accompaniment' is integral to the concept of mentoring.

Mentors share with us the journey through life. Life itself is a sacred journey, from the cradle to the grave, and each life stage brings its own sets of challenges, opportunities and needs. Where we are in life will inevitably have an impact on our walk with God and it is helpful to share the insights of others who have walked the path before us.

Mentors also share the discipleship journey with us. As disciples, we are called to follow Jesus wherever he leads us. We want to seek his will for every aspect of our lives. Sometimes this is straightforward, but at other times we find ourselves at a crossroads, where we can benefit from another person's counsel as we prayerfully weigh up the options.

Mentors can share the inner journey of transformation with us, too, as Christ is formed within us. God is always at work in our lives, using the circumstances of everyday living to shape and mould us. We may not always be able to discern God's hand in events, but others who can see things more objectively can help us to identify how God is at work.

The pilgrim way is not always easy and there are many dangers. It makes good sense, therefore, to find a friend to accompany us along the way.

Prayer

Lord of the journey, thank you for those who share the journey with me.

TH

The Holy Spirit as guide

'All this I have spoken while still with you. But the Counsellor, the Holy Spirit, whom the Father will send in my name, will teach you all things and remind you of everything I have said to you. Peace I leave with you; my peace I give you. I do not give to you as the world gives. Do not let your hearts be troubled and do not be afraid.'

Here, in what we call the upper room discourse (John 14—16), Jesus prepares his disciples for the time when he will no longer be with them. He reassures them with the promise that the Holy Spirit will be their teacher and guide, so they need not be alone or afraid.

In talking about spiritual mentoring, it is important to remember that the true guide is the Holy Spirit. His ministry is to lead us into the truth, taking the things of God and making them real to us (John 16:12–16). He is constantly at work in our lives, helping us to understand new spiritual truths (revelation) and reminding us of what we already know.

The name 'Counsellor' (in Greek, *paracletos*) means 'one who draws alongside to provide help'. Rather like the breakdown services that help stranded motorists, he comes to our aid when we need him most. His ministry is available to all and constantly accessible. In one sense, his ministry of accompaniment is sufficient and we must beware of usurping his place in the life of another believer. The task of a mentor is not to replace the Holy Spirit but to work with him, helping the other person to become more aware of what the Spirit is doing in their life.

Mentoring is therefore a prayerful process, where we are listening to the Holy Spirit and asking him for wisdom. We are not pointing the person to ourselves, but to the Holy Spirit for the help that they need. We seek to encourage the individual into the full blessing of the new covenant: 'No longer will a man teach his neighbour, or a man his brother, saying "Know the Lord", because they will all know me from the least of them to the greatest' (Hebrews 8:11). Our greatest joy should lie in seeing them confidently hear the voice of God for themselves.

Prayer

Holy Spirit, be my guide.

TH

Jesus as mentor

Jesus went up on a mountainside and called to him those he wanted, and they came to him. He appointed twelve—designating them apostles—that they might be with him and that he might send them out to preach and to have authority over demons. These are the twelve he appointed: Simon (to whom he gave the name Peter); James son of Zebedee and his brother John... Andrew, Philip, Bartholomew, Matthew, Thomas, James son of Alphaeus, Thaddeus, Simon the Zealot and Judas Iscariot...

Perhaps the best mandate we have for mentoring others is the example of Jesus. In training the Twelve, he sets before us a pattern of disciple-making in which the mentoring relationship is a key component.

For three years, the disciples had unlimited access to their Master. As they criss-crossed the country with him, they listened to his teaching and had the opportunity to ask him questions about anything they did not understand. They were able to hear his words and see his life at close quarters. They learned from his example as well as his teaching.

Throughout this process, Jesus had two clear objectives. First, that they might be with him. He wanted to share his life with others and being available to them was the best way to inform their minds and shape their characters. Second, he wanted to teach them how to continue his ministry, so that when his earthly life was over his work would continue. Thus, he taught them 'on the job' in a very practical way.

While Jesus often worked with them as a group, he also had time for them as individuals. Perhaps most instructive of all, from a mentoring perspective, is how he dealt with Peter. It would be fair to say that Peter was somewhat 'raw' when he first began to follow Jesus, but the Master saw his potential and stood by him through all his ups and downs. Peter's recommissioning after the resurrection and following his denial is perhaps the most moving illustration of the love that Jesus had for him (John 21:15–19). From a shaky start he had been transformed into the person who would lead the infant Church.

Prayer

Jesus, thank you for calling me and guiding me in your ways.

TH

The benefits of mentoring (1)

There was a man all alone; he had neither son nor brother. There was no end to his toil, yet his eyes were not content with his wealth. 'For whom am I toiling,' he asked, 'and why am I depriving myself of enjoyment?'… Two are better than one, because they have a good return for their work: if they fall down, one can help the other up. But pity those who fall and have no friend to help them up!

Over the next two days, we will consider the benefits of having a soul friend or mentor, using the words of the preacher in Ecclesiastes. Even such a cynic can see the sadness of trying to cope with life without companionship and the wisdom of spiritual friendship.

The first benefit of soul friendship is multiplied effectiveness, or 'synergy'. This is the combined efforts of two people that far outweigh the accomplishments of two individuals working alone. In spiritual terms, when we open our lives to another, our combined ability to discern the will of God is multiplied and we can make much better decisions as a result. By encouraging each other and sharing our knowledge and experience, we can become more effective in our ministry and service.

The second benefit of soul friendship is greater resilience. Challenges come to us all, and in many different ways. Sometimes we may feel overwhelmed with discouragement or crippled by disappointment. At such times it is easy to give up altogether. That is when a soul friend can draw alongside and speak words of faith that help us get back on our feet.

Likewise, temptation is never far away and even the strongest have moments of weakness. When we have sinned and are overtaken by guilt and shame, we need someone who will be there for us, who can speak to us words of grace and forgiveness. In moments of failure and vulnerability, it is especially reassuring to have someone who accepts us as we are, where we are and will gently lead us back on to the right path.

No wonder the Celtic saints used to say that a person without a soul friend is like a body without a head—abnormal and unnatural!

Prayer
Lord, give me friends who will multiply my effectiveness
and increase my resilience.

TH

ECCLESIASTES 4:11–12 (NIV)

The benefits of mentoring (2)

Also, if two lie down together, they will keep warm. But how can one keep warm alone? Though one may be overpowered, two can defend themselves. A cord of three strands is not quickly broken.

We continue to meditate on the wise words of the preacher and his insight into the gift of spiritual friendship.

The third blessing that comes to us through the mentoring relationship is necessary encouragement. Physical warmth will result from sharing a bed with someone, but friendships provide us with the emotional warmth that all of us need. From time to time almost everyone is subject to self-doubt or moments of uncertainty. Even those who appear the most assured and self-sufficient will have times when they will benefit from encouragement. When the storms of adversity hit, we need to be reminded of our security in the love of God. When we are battered by the cold winds of criticism and misunderstanding, we need the protection of those who see our true worth in God.

Finally, mentors provide us with increased protection. We have already mentioned the potential dangers of travelling alone—the greater risks of being mugged or robbed. The Christian life involves us in a spiritual struggle and our souls have an enemy (the devil) who would gladly attack us and steal from us our joy and peace. In times when the battle is fierce and we feel oppressed and subjected to spiritual bombardment, how reassuring it is to have someone who will pray for us and help us to resist the wiles of our enemy! Jesus reminded his followers that there is great power in the prayer of agreement (Matthew 18:18–20).

Spiritual friendship is centred on Jesus, and that reminds us of the strength of the three-fold cord. What holds us together is our mutual love for Christ, and he is the third, and most important, person in the relationship. Aelred of Rievaulx (1109–1167), in his book *Spiritual Friendship*, put it like this: 'Here we are, you and I, and I hope a third—Christ—in our midst.'

Prayer

Lord, you are with me. Grant me also friends who will encourage me with their love and uphold me with their prayers.

TH

Barnabas, son of encouragement

The church at Jerusalem... sent Barnabas to Antioch. When he arrived and saw the evidence of the grace of God, he was glad and encouraged them all to remain true to the Lord with all their hearts. He was a good man, full of the Holy Spirit and faith... Then Barnabas went to Tarsus to look for Saul, and when he found him, he brought him to Antioch. So for a whole year Barnabas and Saul met with the church and taught great numbers of people. The disciples were called Christians first at Antioch.

Today we remember Barnabas, one of the great figures of the early Church. Barnabas models what it means be a mentor, to come alongside someone to help them grow in faith. After Saul's dramatic conversion, Barnabas had introduced him to the leaders of the Jerusalem church, but, under threat of persecution, Saul had withdrawn to Tarsus. Some people were still suspicious of him (Acts 9:21) and perhaps he was discouraged. Certainly he needed time to think through his newfound faith and how it was different from the Judaism of his former life.

Seeing the great opportunity developing in Antioch, Barnabas went and found Saul, then brought him back to help in the teaching ministry that was blossoming and for which his gifts ideally suited him. This is one of the great moments in church history. What if Saul had been allowed to disappear for good? It took the heart of a Barnabas to see the potential in a person like Saul, draw him gently back into ministry and give him the chance to develop his gift. This is mentoring at its best.

It seems appropriate today to think also of BRF's *Barnabas* ministry. Through books and resources, RE days and classroom teaching, the *Barnabas* team members aim to help children in schools on their spiritual journey. They also work in churches to nurture the faith of those children already within a church context. Who knows what potential lies hidden in the lives of the young people they meet and influence?

Barnabas looked for Saul and found him. It required risk-taking, initiative and, above all, the love that believes in the potential of others.

Prayer
Lord, make us sons and daughters of encouragement.

TH

2 TIMOTHY 2:1–3 (NIV)

Paul, father in the faith

You then, my son, be strong in the grace that is in Christ Jesus. And the things you have heard me say in the presence of many witnesses entrust to reliable people who will also be qualified to teach others. Endure hardship with us like a good soldier of Christ Jesus.

Now we see that Barnabas' strategy of developing others through mentoring was at the heart of Paul's own apostolic ministry.

As we read the New Testament, it is noticeable that Paul instinctively gathered around him people with potential whom he trained and developed—Silas, Titus, Epaphroditus, Luke and, of course, Timothy. His principle was simple: multiply the Church by investing time in developing key people who, in turn, can develop others and so on.

Paul had a particular regard for young Timothy, whom he met during his first missionary journey (Acts 16:1–3) and who became a kind of spiritual apprentice. Wherever Paul went, Timothy followed, learning on the job as they travelled. Sometimes he would be sent to deal with difficult church situations that arose (1 Corinthians 4:17) and, eventually, he was placed in charge of the church at Ephesus (1 Timothy 1:3).

Timothy was not a natural leader, being somewhat shy (2 Timothy 1:6–7), but Paul recognised his faithfulness and his great desire for God. The two letters Paul wrote to encourage Timothy in his ministry reflect his love for one whom he regarded as a son, and they are filled with the wisdom that continues to inspire church leaders today. Knowing Timothy and his particular needs, Paul is able to point him to the grace of God, which is sufficient for him in all situations, and keep encouraging him to move forwards on the path of discipleship.

It has been said that everyone should have a Paul, a Barnabas and a Timothy in their life—someone older and wiser to guide them; a good friend to stand alongside and encourage them; and a younger person around them whom they can develop. That in essence is how mentoring works and it makes for a healthy, growing church.

Prayer
Lord, thank you for those who have touched my life for the good and helped me to grow in faith.

TH

Facing our fears

Again the Israelites did evil in the eyes of the Lord, and for seven years he gave them into the hands of the Midianites... The angel of the Lord came and sat down under the oak in Ophrah that belonged to Joash the Abiezrite, where his son Gideon was thresh-ing wheat in a winepress to keep it from the Midianites. When the angel of the Lord appeared to Gideon, he said, 'The Lord is with you, mighty warrior.'

We look now in detail at an example of mentoring: the story of Gideon's encounter with the 'angel of the Lord'.

The 'angel of the Lord' is a mysterious figure whom many commen-tators regard as a pre-incarnational appearance of Christ. Certainly we shall see that Gideon responds as if he is speaking to a divine person. It is interesting to note how carefully the angel guides the conversation so that the young man is helped to realise his divine destiny. He comes to Gideon at his place of work and quietly observes him before delivering his message: 'The Lord is with you, mighty warrior.'

One of the primary objectives of mentoring is helping people to see themselves as God sees them, to recognise his call in their lives and to step into their God-given destiny. For this to happen, any hindrances holding them back have to be dealt with. For Gideon, the first of these was his fearfulness. Israel had been under Midianite rule for seven long years. Every harvest, Midianite raiders would sweep in and steal the crops, plundering and murdering on the way. That is why Gideon is hiding away in the wine press. It was not the most sensible place to thresh wheat, but probably the safest. Like his contemporaries, Gideon lived in daily fear for his life and he felt anything but a mighty warrior.

We all have fears and hiding places. We may shrink from doing God's will because we are afraid of failure or of what others may say. A men-tor's task is to help us identify our fears and replace them with faith—the belief that God has a unique role for each of us within his kingdom.

Prayer

Lord, give us confidence, so that we may really believe that you can use us to achieve your purposes through our lives.

TH

Processing our questions

'But sir,' Gideon replied, 'if the Lord is with us, why has all this happened to us? Where are all his wonders that our fathers told us about when they said, "Did not the Lord bring us up out of Egypt?" But now the Lord has abandoned us and put us into the hand of Midian.' The Lord... said, 'Go in the strength you have and save Israel out of Midian's hand. Am I not sending you?'

Once Gideon finds his voice, he has much to ask, and his perplexity and frustration pour out. 'If the Lord is with us, why has all this happened to us?' It is a common question that many of us have asked at various times. We wonder why bad things happen to good people and, just as disturbingly, why good things happen to bad people. It just seems so unfair! The confusing events of life challenge our theology and cause deep heart-searching for even the most godly among us.

'Where are all his wonders?' Stories of God's past deeds may be inspiring, but when nothing is happening in the present, they can be counter-productive, highlighting our own disappointment with God. We wonder why God doesn't answer our prayers and why we see little response to the gospel. We may feel that we work hard for little reward and—if we are really honest—find that we are annoyed with God.

'But now the Lord has abandoned us.' Here is the sad sense that God has withdrawn not only his blessing but also his presence. It describes a spiritual darkness that some experience on their spiritual journey and raises questions that need answers. Why does God seem so far away? Why is his presence so elusive?

Interestingly, the angel does not respond directly to his queries. Mentors must beware of offering pat answers to deep questions. Sometimes, as Henri Nouwen said, we must choose to live the questions, leaving our perplexity with God, allowing time and greater reflection to mature our thinking.

Reflection

Even our questions are part of the journey and our searching can be used to help others. The main thing is to remember that God is with us. 'Am I not sending you?' is a question to override all other questions.

TH

Overcoming our insecurities

'But Lord,' Gideon asked, 'how can I save Israel? My clan is the weakest in Manasseh, and I am the least in my family.' The Lord answered, 'I will be with you, and you will strike down all the Midianites together.'

With each phase of the dialogue, the conversation deepens and the issues become more pertinent. Gideon is now drawn to focus on his deep-seated sense of inadequacy: 'How can I save Israel?' he asks despairingly.

Humility is a good quality to have, as is a sense of our own weakness, but what Gideon is facing here is more like a crippling sense of inferiority. His personal history is the root of his trouble. He is from the tribe of Manasseh, one of the least well regarded in Israel. Furthermore, he is from the weakest clan within that tribe, the Abiezrites. To make matters even worse, his family are the least influential within their clan and Gideon is the least (possibly youngest) within his family. In other words, he is at the bottom of the pile and he knows it.

How often we destroy our sense of worth by comparing ourselves negatively to others! We may regard ourselves as being less well-educated, less well-off, less well-spoken, less gifted, less popular, less attractive and so on. Often this sense of inadequacy holds us back from entering fully into everything that God would have us do and be.

The angel points Gideon away from his preoccupation with self, moving his gaze to where it rightly belongs—on the one who is calling him and will enable him. 'I will be with you,' says the angel—healing and liberating words of promise and of presence that carry the assurance of victory. 'You will strike down all the Midianites together.'

Mentors remind us of the fundamental truth that our identity is found in God, not in our achievements or performance. We have worth because we were made by God to know him and work in partnership with him. We have value because God gave his Son to die for us.

Reflection

We need to return to these foundational truths time and again, so that our sense of inadequacy does not undermine our calling.

TH

JUDGES 6:17–18 (NIV)

Dealing with our uncertainties

Gideon replied, 'If now I have found favour in your eyes, give me a sign that it is really you talking to me. Please do not go away until I come back and bring my offering and set it before you.' And the Lord said, 'I will wait until you return.'

The 'angel of the Lord' has gently guided Gideon through a process of self-discovery and recognition of the calling of God. It has been like peeling away the layers of an onion, as the work of grace in his life has gone deeper. Now he is faced with his uncertainties.

The first uncertainty is whether or not he is worthy of divine favour. 'If now I have found favour in your eyes,' he says hesitantly. After his initial reluctance, bold questioning and slowness of response, surely he has forfeited God's favour? Isn't that the reward of the strong, not the weak like him? Grace, by definition, is for the undeserving, but, like Gideon, we may feel disqualified from receiving God's blessing.

The second uncertainty is whether or not it is in fact the voice of God that he is hearing. 'Give me a sign that it is really you talking to me,' he pleads. This is one issue that troubles many Christians. How do we know when God is speaking to us? Isn't it just our imagination? Maybe we are simply imagining what we want to hear? Such doubts commonly assail us when we long to hear God for ourselves.

The angel's response is just what Gideon needs. He is prepared to give Gideon time and space. 'I will wait for you,' he says, with gracious condescension. God is never in a hurry. Patience is also one of the important qualities of a mentor, for we cannot rush the work of God in the life of another. When Gideon finally presents the offering, the angel touches it with his staff and it is consumed (v. 21). This miraculous sign bolsters Gideon's faith and now his doubt has gone. Uncertainty is replaced by the revelation that he has encountered Jehovah-Shalom—the Lord is peace (v. 24).

Reflection

Mentors can never take the place of God and are dependent on God
to reveal himself. Their job is to patiently guide the process,
waiting for God to act in grace.

TH

Holy listening

Every good and perfect gift is from above, coming down from the Father... who does not change like shifting shadows... My dear brothers and sisters, take note of this: everyone should be quick to listen, slow to speak and slow to become angry, for human anger does not bring about the righteous life that God desires.

Sitting next to a businessman at a dinner, I listened as he told me about himself and his troubles, although we had never met before. Suddenly he stopped and, turning to me, said, 'But why am I telling you all this?' 'Perhaps because I am listening', I replied.

Attentive listening is one of the main gifts we are able to give to others in the mentoring process. Indeed, it is one of the most valuable gifts we can ever give to another person because too few people have had the experience of being truly listened to and, equally, few of us know how to listen well. When we do find someone who gives us their attention, we feel valued and affirmed and so most of us take the opportunity to talk, usually saying more than we intended and in a deeper way. That is why listening is a very healing gift.

I always assumed that because I was in a pastoral ministry I was a good listener. It was only when I attended a course on listening skills that I realised I wasn't so good after all. In fact, to me, 'listening' turned out to be simply waiting for my turn to speak. I often assumed that I knew where the conversation was going and what the other person needed to hear. In my mind I was already composing my reply before he or she had finished speaking! I'm glad to say that I have developed my listening skills since then.

Listening requires us to give our full attention to what the other person is saying, so we have to tune out our own thoughts in order to concentrate on what we are hearing. It is not about giving advice or sharing stories, so when we are truly listening we say very little. We may ask an occasional question for clarification or to open up an area for further exploration, but listening is, in essence, the gift of not talking.

Prayer
Lord, teach me to listen.

TH

Holy conversations

Then those who feared the Lord talked with each other, and the Lord listened and heard. A scroll of remembrance was written in his presence concerning those who feared the Lord and honoured his name. 'They will be mine,' says the Lord Almighty, 'in the day when I make up my treasured possession. I will spare them, just as in compassion parents spare their children who serve them.'

Malachi is writing during a period of spiritual decline in Israel and his aim is to restore the nation's spiritual vitality. One remedy is to encourage God's people to talk about spiritual issues without embarrassment.

All too often we are afraid to share deeply with each other, even in the context of Christian fellowship. If we are to encourage each other to press on in our faith, though, we must be able to talk openly about the things that really matter. We have been thinking about mentoring as a one-to-one relationship, but the principles can be applied to a group that is meeting specifically for the purpose of spiritual friendship.

The members of such a group can get together with some clear guidelines in mind—to share openly with each other about their spiritual journey, listen respectfully and prayerfully to what is shared, welcome questions without giving easy answers and listen to what God may be saying to the group. Such a group need only meet once a month, yet can expect that, over a period of time, deep relationships will be formed that will nurture their spiritual growth further.

Sometimes it is helpful to have a few questions in mind that can serve to open up spiritual conversation. 'How is your relationship with God at this moment?' or 'How have you seen God at work in your life since we last met?' are simple examples. Some groups may want to encourage one person each time to share the story of their spiritual journey and to follow this with prayer. There is no set formula; a group can make its own pattern according to its members.

Malachi tells us that God loves such 'holy conversations'. It pleases him when we open our hearts to one another. He listens and he hears.

Prayer

Lord, show me how I can join with others to talk about you.

TH

Bible stories rediscovered:
creation and fall

Just as the roots of a mighty oak tree plunge deep through the soil, securing it into the bedrock itself, so Genesis anchors, supports and nourishes all that unfurls in the rest of scripture. Our first impression is of a disparate collection of material. There are various genres and sources; different perspectives on the same event sit side by side; poetry, genealogies and various kinds of narratives are woven together into a multicoloured tapestry. On closer inspection, though, recurring patterns appear, joined by threads that continue throughout the Bible.

Genesis represents the beginning of a covenant that binds together God, his people and the wider creation. The establishment of this promise-based relationship is a presupposition for all that follows in the Bible. The opening chapters mark a radical break with an ancient view that saw the gods as open to human control and manipulation. The tendency of flawed humans to fabricate gods in their own image continues to the present day. Genesis both explains the root of this temptation and challenges any diminished or distorted view of the Creator.

As we allow Genesis to shape our worldview, the idea of God as a benevolent but disinterested clockmaker—setting his creation in motion and leaving it to its own devices—will be challenged. Equally, any concept of God as a puppeteer and us as helpless puppets will be confronted. Rather, we find him to be intimately involved in his world and yet he gives us freedom to accept his loving guidance or to reject it.

The nature of our humanity, paradoxical and complex, is also explored. Created in the image of God, we should never doubt our dignity and value. Equally, flawed and prone to disobedience, we should never be surprised at the depths to which we can sink. Within a few short chapters we see how harmony between environment, each other and God descends into jealousy and conflict between siblings. The continuous circle of love binding Creator and creation is shattered. Pain, deceit and murder enter the world as a consequence.

There is hope, however! The golden threads of covenant and blessing remain and, as full-blown rebellion against God emerges, so does a counter-culture—a remnant of faithful worshippers, eager to align their ways with his and hopeful of redemption.

Steve Aisthorpe

On the origin of everything

In the beginning God created the heavens and the earth. Now the earth was formless and empty, darkness was over the surface of the deep, and the Spirit of God was hovering over the waters. And God said, 'Let there be light', and there was light. God saw that the light was good, and he separated the light from the darkness. God called the light 'day', and the darkness he called 'night'. And there was evening, and there was morning—the first day.

A four-year-old boy asked his mother, somewhat hesitantly, 'Where did I come from?' His mother, thinking it was a little early for explanations but wanting to respond with appropriate gravity, described as simply as possible the biology involved. The boy looked amazed and replied with a frown, 'Oh… my friend James says he came from Manchester'!

When it comes to interpreting the God-breathed, poetic narrative that opens the Bible, there is a danger of wrestling with issues that are not being addressed. The primary concern of the writer of Genesis was not the *how* or the *when* of creation but, rather, the *who*. These opening verses lay a foundation for all that follows. The psalmist later summarised it thus: 'Know this: GOD is God, and God, GOD. He made us; we didn't make him' (Psalm 100:3, *THE MESSAGE*).

Making gods in our own image is not just a modern phenomenon. Ancient myths were full of gods of limited power and temperamental character, prone to tantrums and unpredictable reprisals. Genesis mounts a radical challenge to any belief system, scientific or mythological, that attempts to address questions of life without reference to God.

'There's probably no God. Now stop worrying and enjoy your life.' So read the controversial slogan on UK buses and the London Underground in 2009. Yet the book that points the way to 'life in all its fullness' (John 10:10, GNB) and a joy-filled life free from anxiety (Philippians 4:4–7) begins with the phrase, 'In the beginning… God' (v. 1).

Reflection

The God of Creation is the guarantee of Order, the repudiation of Accident or Chance' (H.C. Brichto, The Names of God, OUP, p. 397). Thank the Lord for an ordered and purposeful world and for his loving presence.

SA

GENESIS 1:9–13 (NIV)

Good? Suffering in context

And God said, 'Let the water under the sky be gathered to one place, and let dry ground appear.' And it was so. God called the dry ground 'land', and the gathered waters he called 'seas'. And God saw that it was good. Then God said, 'Let the land produce vegetation: seed-bearing plants and trees on the land that bear fruit with seed in it, according to their various kinds.' And it was so. The land produced vegetation: plants bearing seed according to their kinds and trees bearing fruit with seed in it according to their kinds. And God saw that it was good. And there was evening, and there was morning—the third day.

'Life is difficult.' So begins M. Scott Peck's book, *The Road Less Travelled* (Rider, 2008). Most of us have enough proof of that in our own lives: tragic accidents occur, illness robs us of well-being, the processes of decay inherent in ageing take their toll. If our own experience provides insufficient evidence, we only need to hear the news broadcasts: poverty, environmental disasters and so-called 'acts of God' wreak havoc and the foundations of our own society appear to be crumbling.

What, then, do we make of God's sevenfold affirmation of every aspect of creation, 'It was good'? The truth is that all suffering in this world takes place during the phase of life that occurs between the absolute perfection of original creation and the complete restoration of that flawless creation still to come (Isaiah 25:8; Revelation 21:4). The apostle Paul was able to see his own suffering from this perspective. The same Paul who was flogged, stoned and shipwrecked was able to say, 'I consider that our present sufferings are not worth comparing with the glory that will be revealed in us' (Romans 8:18).

Yes, life is difficult, but it will not always be so. In the meantime, Christ promises comfort to those who mourn (Matthew 5:4), rest for the weary (Matthew 11:28) and peace for all who trust in him: 'Do not let your hearts be troubled and do not be afraid' (John 14:27).

Prayer

Creator God, thank you for your promise of restoration. Please strengthen and comfort all who suffer. May I be a channel of your compassion. Amen

SA

1 + 1 + 1 = 1

Then God said, 'Let us make human beings in our image, in our likeness, and let them rule over the fish of the sea and the birds of the air, over the livestock, over all the earth, and over all the creatures that move along the ground.' So God created human beings in his own image, in the image of God he created them; male and female he created them.

I was at a remote, unstaffed Highland station, hoping to take my bicycle on a northbound train. A southbound train arrived and I asked the guard about this. I'll never forget his answer: 'You'll need to ask the guard on the northbound train.' Then, as he hopped on to the departing train, 'It'll be myself!' Later, the northbound train arrived. Sure enough, the guard was 'himself', one and the same but in a different role. My bike and I were welcomed aboard!

Today's passage gives us astounding insights into both humanity and the nature of God. Just as I stood bewildered on that station, so a first reading of verse 26 leaves us wondering: 'us… our… our'? Is there some plurality in the character of God? This first hint is reinforced by mysterious references later in Genesis (3:22; 11:7). The prophets have tantalising glimpses of God's 'three-in-oneness'. Isaiah talks of the Holy Spirit (63:10–14) and John says that Isaiah 'saw Jesus' glory' (12:41). The New Testament writers unpack much more of the mysterious truth that we call the Trinity: God's distinguishable persons, yet perfect unity.

If the notion of plurality in the Godhead were not enough, the writer of Genesis tells us that this awesome God created us 'in his own image'. It is impossible to plumb the depths of all that this implies and it is a theme to which we shall return. One implication is that the unity, harmony and love that characterise relationships within the Godhead are his desire and purpose for us.

Reflection

God's aim in human history is the creation of an inclusive community of loving persons, with himself as its primary sustainer and most glorious inhabitant.

Dallas Willard, quoted in Richard Foster, *Celebration of Discipline*, p. 162

SA

From exploitation to stewardship

God blessed them and said to them, 'Be fruitful and increase in number; fill the earth and subdue it. Rule over the fish of the sea and the birds of the air and over every living creature that moves on the ground.' Then God said, 'I give you every seed-bearing plant on the face of the whole earth and every tree that has fruit with seed in it. They will be yours for food.'

The headlines scream it, governments recognise it—there is a growing consensus that we face an unprecedented environmental crisis. We are waking up to issues of climate change, depletion of the ozone layer, extinction of species and the degradation of air and water.

Amid the debates, misunderstanding of today's passage is sometimes cited as being responsible for engendering an unhealthy attitude towards this amazing planet that we call home. The thinking on words such as 'subdue' and 'rule over' has sometimes led to the view that all creation is for our benefit and revolves around us. David saw it differently: 'The earth is the Lord's, and everything in it' (Psalm 24:1).

A misunderstanding that this earth is destined for destruction, coupled with the biblical promises that the Lord will create a new earth ('so why bother about this world?') has undermined the view of God's people as its stewards. There will be a new earth, but that means 'new' in terms of quality; the new creation will be part of God's transformation (Revelation 21—22).

Ancient kings set up images of themselves throughout their territory as a symbol of their rule. Being made in the image of God, we have a delegated authority over creation. THE MESSAGE renders Genesis 1:26 as, 'Let us make human beings in our image, make them reflecting our nature so they can be responsible for the fish in the sea, the birds in the air, the cattle, and, yes, Earth itself…'. We are to be stewards, exercising responsibility with care and compassion.

Reflection

The Bible doesn't begin with sin and end at the cross. Rather, it begins with a perfect creation and ends, by way of the resurrection, with a perfect new creation. Ask the Lord what it might mean for you to be a better steward.

SA

GENESIS 1:31—2:3 (NIV)

Stop!

God saw all that he had made, and it was very good. And there was evening, and there was morning—the sixth day. Thus the heavens and the earth were completed in all their vast array. By the seventh day God had finished the work he had been doing; so on the seventh day he rested from all his work. And God blessed the seventh day and made it holy, because on it he rested from all the work of creating that he had done.

A small aircraft was flying from the Midwest in the USA to the East Coast. During the flight it became apparent to the ground controllers that the pilot was not flying according to the filed flight plan. All efforts to communicate with him failed: unbeknown to them, both pilot and passenger were unconscious because of an oxygen supply failure. Because the plane was on autopilot, however, it flew on. Eventually it headed out to sea—flying on and on until it ran out of fuel and fell from the air. To the uninformed observer everything looked fine… until it eventually plunged into the sea.

In our 24/7 culture, this tragic flight might be a poignant analogy for the lives some of us lead. Many jobs do not give the satisfaction of having truly finished a task. We can feel as if we are on a treadmill, with none of the ebb and flow that characterised the life of Christ (Mark 6:31; Luke 5:16), no pause for thanksgiving and well-earned rest—just relentless grind until we make it to the next holiday or burn out.

God initiated the sabbath as part of the divine order for creation. It was to be a model for all time and all people, a principle of such foundational importance that God put it in the Ten Commandments (Exodus 20:8–11). The Bible tells us little about what we are to do on the sabbath, but, when we respect it and find ways to express our gratitude and love to our Creator, we will find our souls are nourished and our joy replenished.

Prayer

Almighty Creator, loving Father, thank you for your wise and gracious exhortations. Please help me to be faithful in my expression of the sabbath principle—both for myself and in the expectations I have of others. Amen

SA

The perennial question

When the Lord God made the earth and the heavens—and no shrub of the field had yet appeared on the earth... for the Lord God had not sent rain on the earth and there was no man to work the ground, but streams came up from the earth and watered the whole surface of the ground—the Lord God formed the man from the dust of the ground and breathed into his nostrils the breath of life, and the man became a living being.

The average body contains about 6.7×10^{27} atoms; 99 per cent of our body is made up of just six elements; there's enough carbon to make 900 pencils, ample fat to make several bars of soap and sufficient phosphorus to make 2200 match heads. At a purely physical level, we have never known more about what it means to be human, yet the psalmist's question, 'What is man... ?' (Psalm 8:4) continues to confront us with a pressing urgency.

The opening paragraphs of Genesis provide a foundation for understanding the paradox of humanness. Like the animals, we are living creatures made from the dust of the ground (Genesis 2:7, 19). At the same time, we are formed uniquely in the 'image' and 'likeness' of God (1:26–27). In the passage above, we see life bestowed in a personal, face-to-face encounter between Creator and creation that is paralleled by the action of Jesus as he brought new life to his disciples: 'he breathed on them and said, "Receive the Holy Spirit"' (John 20:22).

We exist because God made us, as a race and as individuals (Jeremiah 1:5), and, while we are flawed by sin, we are still bearers of God's image. It is this that distinguishes us as those with the capacity to love and be loved. Sense the note of awe and reverence in the ponderings of David: 'What is man that you are mindful of him, the son of man that you care for him? You made him a little lower than the heavenly beings and crowned him with glory and honour' (Psalm 8:4–5).

Prayer

Lord, in quietness, humility and with deep reverence, I thank you for making me. Please grow your character in me and give me the wisdom and love to enjoy you and serve you with my whole being. Amen

SA

GENESIS 2:8–9, 15 (NIV)

Drudgery or devotion?

Now the Lord God had planted a garden in the east, in Eden; and there he put the man he had formed. And the Lord God made all kinds of trees grow out of the ground—trees that were pleasing to the eye and good for food. In the middle of the garden were the tree of life and the tree of the knowledge of good and evil... The Lord God took the man and put him in the Garden of Eden to work it and take care of it.

Gardening requires lots of water—most of it in the form of sweat! In placing that first man in the garden, God inaugurated his first calling: work. There is no hint of any negative connotation here, though. The name 'Eden' comes from the Hebrew word meaning 'delight'. Work was an integral part of man's enjoyment of that delight. Later, following human disobedience, work took on a frustrating character, but even then work remained his calling (3:17–19).

It is fashionable to denigrate work: we often express a commonly held view of work as a necessary evil. The Bible, while leaving us in no doubt that God abhors exploitation, also maintains that work has dignity and should be carried out as an offering to the Lord: 'Whatever you do, work at it with all your heart, as working for the Lord, not for human masters' (Colossians 3:23).

Brother Lawrence (1614–1691), a Carmelite monk, spent much of his life working in kitchens and repairing sandals. These apparently mundane tasks were transformed by a realisation that they were to be the medium of his worship. His insights were later recorded in *The Practice of the Presence of God*—a book that has influenced Christians of every generation since and speaks powerfully to our contemporary culture. Most of us will spend about half of our lives working or in work-related activities. Whether that time is worship or drudgery is largely our choice.

Prayer

Take my life, and let it be consecrated, Lord, to thee;
Take my moments and my days, let them flow in ceaseless praise.

Frances R. Havergal (1836–1879)

SA

The same... but different

The Lord God said, 'It is not good for the man to be alone. I will make a helper suitable for him.'... So the Lord God caused the man to fall into a deep sleep... took one of the man's ribs and closed up the place with flesh. Then the Lord God made a woman from the rib he had taken out of the man, and he brought her to the man. The man said, 'This is now bone of my bones and flesh of my flesh; she shall be called "woman", for she was taken out of man.'

Once upon a time, Martians and Venusians fell in love and had happy relationships together. They respected and accepted their differences. Then they came to earth and forgot they were from different planets!

Don't worry, I haven't gone totally off the rails—this is the metaphor that John Gray uses in his bestselling book, *Men are from Mars, Women are from Venus* (Harper, 1993). Our need to understand gender is crucial to harmonious living, a point highlighted by the fact that few books have sold more copies during the last decade than those of Dr Gray. While his books do not attempt to be biblical, they do contain important kernels of truth regarding the different but complementary natures of men and women.

The New Testament writers looked on Genesis 2 as a foundation for understanding the sexes. Man is revealed as having social needs; he is made for fellowship (v. 18). The creation of one who is 'the same, but different' is God's response. Adam is overjoyed at the degree of similarity: 'At last!... This is bone from my bone, and flesh from my flesh!' (v. 23, NLT). The similarity is balanced by complementarity, however. The term 'suitable helper' (vv. 18, 20) literally means 'a help opposite him' or 'corresponding to him'. There is no hint of any difference in status, only of compatibility, interdependence and companionship.

Reflection

She was not created from his head to be above him; nor was she created from his foot to be trampled by him. She was taken from his side to be his equal, from beneath his arm to be protected by him, from near his heart to be loved by him.

Author unknown

SA

GENESIS 3:1–6 (NIV)

Standing firm? Be careful

Now the serpent was more crafty than any of the wild animals the Lord God had made. He said to the woman, 'Did God really say, "You must not eat from any tree in the garden"?' The woman said to the serpent, 'We may eat fruit from the trees in the garden, but God did say, "You must not eat fruit from the tree that is in the middle of the garden, and you must not touch it, or you will die."' 'You will not surely die,' the serpent said to the woman. 'For God knows that when you eat of it your eyes will be opened, and you will be like God, knowing good and evil.' When the woman saw that the fruit of the tree was good for food and pleasing to the eye, and also desirable for gaining wisdom, she took some and ate it. She also gave some to her husband, who was with her, and he ate it.

Into a situation of shameless innocence (2:25) comes the tempter. He comes not with abrasive arguments or lavish claims, but with a gentle suggestion: 'Did God really say...?' Tactic two is exaggeration: 'You must not eat from *any* tree in the garden?' (3:1). Eve is hooked and she adds her own subtle exaggeration: 'and you must not touch it, or you will die' (v. 3). Finally, after sowing seeds of doubt about God's character, the full-blown contradiction comes: 'You will not surely die' (v. 4).

It is a strategy that has worked throughout history. Our heavenly Father, 'the compassionate and gracious God, slow to anger, abounding in love and faithfulness' (Exodus 34:6), is portrayed as a megalomaniac, prone to petty jealousy. Humanity's privileged and dignified role as servants of the almighty Creator is portrayed as sycophancy or misguided self-enslavement. The path to broken fellowship with God, guilt and shame, is disguised as the route to a richer, fuller life.

Jesus faced the same kinds of tests as Adam and Eve, but overcame them. Now he helps *us* to overcome: 'when you are tempted, he will also provide a way out so that you can stand up under it' (1 Corinthians 10:13).

Prayer

Father, I want to live for you today. Please give me the courage and wisdom to overcome every temptation to doubt your holy, gracious character. Amen

SA

Hide and seek

Then the eyes of both of them were opened, and they realised they were naked; so they sewed fig leaves together and made coverings for themselves. Then the man and his wife heard the sound of the Lord God as he was walking in the garden in the cool of the day, and they hid from the Lord God among the trees of the garden. But the Lord God called to the man, 'Where are you?'

So begins the ultimate tale of hide and seek. The Bible is full of people on the run: Hagar, Jacob, Jonah, and even the first disciples, who deserted Jesus and fled (Mark 14:50). Hiding from God is part of the human condition, as Francis Thompson wrote in 'The hound of heaven':

> *I fled Him, down the labyrinthine ways*
> *Of my own mind; and in the mist of tears*
> *I hid from Him, and under running laughter.*

The 'hound of heaven' pursues us not with the relentless chase and forceful overcoming of a hunter, however, but with the persistent seeking and costly rescuing of the good shepherd: 'I will search for the lost and bring back the strays' (Ezekiel 34:16).

When Jesus was accused of 'welcoming sinners', he answered with three parables, all found in Luke 15. The parable of the lost sheep tells of his deep concern for the individual (vv. 3–7). The lost coin speaks of a diligent, patient search (vv. 8–10). The lost son (some would say, 'sons', as both sons in the story were lost in their own ways) explains the extravagant and gracious welcome that awaits the one who 'was lost, but now is found' (vv. 11–31). Jesus' attitude is clear: not only does he welcome sinners, he seeks them out. It started in Eden and goes on to this day. Our invitation is to 'Seek the Lord while he may be found' (Isaiah 55:6); our commission is to ensure that this invitation is widely known (Matthew 28:18–20).

Reflection

'But while he was still a long way off, his father saw him and was filled with compassion for him; he ran to his son, threw his arms around him and kissed him' (Luke 15:20).

SA

The sting of death

To the woman [God] said, 'I will greatly increase your pains in childbearing; with pain you will give birth to children. Your desire will be for your husband, and he will rule over you.' To Adam he said, 'Because you listened to your wife and ate from the tree about which I commanded you, "You must not eat of it", cursed is the ground because of you; through painful toil you will eat of it all the days of your life. It will produce thorns and thistles for you, and you will eat the plants of the field. By the sweat of your brow you will eat your food until you return to the ground, since from it you were taken; for dust you are and to dust you will return.'

Endurance athletes become 'habituated' to pain: they develop a tolerance of pain as they experience it daily. Living in a world where pain, physical and emotional, is a present reality, we all, to some degree, become habituated to its presence and impact. Similarly, we become used to the muted daylight of a cloudy day, but when a cloud crosses the sun, we immediately shiver at the sudden change. We can sense an abrupt change in today's passage, too.

Naked and ashamed, the man and woman reluctantly emerge from hiding. Everything has changed: the previous harmony is gone. The loving fellowship between Adam and Eve and their Maker has been replaced by a cold, awkward estrangement. It is the low point in human history, one to which all other tragedies and horrors since can trace their roots. The joy of motherhood is tainted with pain and anxiety (vv. 15–16). Satisfying labour becomes frustrating toil (vv. 18–19). 'To love and cherish' becomes 'to desire and dominate' (v. 16). Life will now be lived in the shadow of death (v. 19).

Fortunately, while we still live in an era when all beauty is tainted, we also glimpse the hope of a new era. Our pain is like that of childbirth: it points us forward to the time when creation will be liberated from decay (Romans 8:21–22), when death, mourning and pain will be no more.

Reflection
While we live in the shadow, we are a post-Easter people—
death has lost its sting. Hallelujah!

SA

Compassion leads to action

The Lord God made garments of skin for Adam and his wife and clothed them. And the Lord God said, 'The man has now become like one of us, knowing good and evil. He must not be allowed to... take also from the tree of life and eat, and live for ever.' So the Lord God banished him from the Garden of Eden to work the ground from which he had been taken. After he drove the man out, he placed on the east side of the Garden of Eden cherubim and a flaming sword... to guard the way to the tree of life.

Gutted, devastated, distraught—Adam and Eve must have missed and yearned for the warmth and depth of intimacy with God that had characterised Eden. Yet that tender act of clothing them must have also spoken profoundly of the unconditional, if pained, love of their Father.

The impact of Adam and Eve's banishment has rolled down the ages. The fact that we are 'children of Adam' gives us a feeling of homesickness. We have a taste of the exclusion that Adam and Eve first experienced as they went east of Eden. We know, however, that we are also 'dearly loved children' of God who have been commanded to 'be imitators' of him (Ephesians 5:1). One aspect of that is learning and developing some of God's practical compassion: 'The Lord God made garments of skin for Adam and his wife and clothed them' (Genesis 3:21).

Despite the chasm that has opened between God and his creation, he remains, eternally, 'the compassionate... God' (Exodus 34:6). Compassion is a noun that longs to be a verb: wherever we find it applied to God or Jesus, it results in action. Our merciful acts are commended by scripture: 'I needed clothes and you clothed me' (Matthew 25:36). Neglect of mercy suggests that our faith is defective: 'Suppose a brother or sister is without clothes and daily food. If one of you says to him, "Go, I wish you well; keep warm and well fed," but does nothing about his physical needs, what good is it? In the same way, faith by itself, if it is not accompanied by action, is dead' (James 2:15–17).

Prayer

Lord, please open my eyes to opportunities to demonstrate your practical love today. Amen

SA

True worship

Adam lay with his wife Eve, and she… gave birth to Cain… Later she gave birth to his brother Abel. Now Abel kept flocks, and Cain worked the soil. In the course of time Cain brought some of the fruits of the soil as an offering to the Lord. But Abel brought fat portions from some of the firstborn of his flock. The Lord looked with favour on Abel and his offering, but on Cain and his offering he did not look with favour. So Cain was very angry, and his face was downcast. Then the Lord said to Cain, 'Why are you angry?… If you do what is right, will you not be accepted? But if you do not do what is right, sin is crouching at your door… you must master it.' Now Cain said to his brother Abel, 'Let's go out to the field.' And while they were in the field, Cain attacked his brother Abel and killed him.

Like ripples radiating out from a pebble dropped into a pond, the infectious consequences of Eve and Adam's disobedience pursue the generations that follow. Callous sibling rivalries are a feature of Genesis—Cain and Abel, Ishmael and Isaac, Jacob and Esau. The helter-skelter spiral of sin takes its course: 'after desire has conceived, it gives birth to sin; and sin, when it is full-grown, gives birth to death' (James 1:15).

Genesis gives us few clues as to why Abel's offering was acceptable and Cain's was not. We need to look to the New Testament for those. It appears to have had everything to do with the attitudes of the worshippers. Abel is celebrated as a man of faith, his offering reflecting a genuine and whole-hearted gratitude to the Lord (Hebrews 11:4), whereas Cain is condemned for his self-seeking motives (Jude 11).

Worship is not synonymous with singing hymns and songs, although doing so may be a valuable part of it. As Paul writes, believers are called to 'offer your bodies as living sacrifices, holy and pleasing to God—this is your spiritual act of worship' (Romans 12:1). We are not to be consumers of worship experiences. Rather, we are to bring to God our whole being as an unreserved, unconditional, heartfelt thanks offering to him.

Prayer

Father, here I am. May all I do and think and say be pleasing to you. Amen

SA

Choices beget consequences

Cain lay with his wife, and she became pregnant and gave birth to Enoch. Cain was then building a city, and he named it after his son Enoch... Lamech said to his wives, 'Adah and Zillah, listen to me; wives of Lamech, hear my words. I have killed a man for wounding me, a young man for injuring me. If Cain is avenged seven times, then Lamech seventy-seven times.' Adam lay with his wife again, and she gave birth to a son and named him Seth, saying, 'God has granted me another child in place of Abel, since Cain killed him.' Seth also had a son, and he named him Enosh. At that time people began to call on the name of the Lord.

The 1998 film *Sliding Doors* explores the potentially huge impacts of apparently small life choices. Two parallel stories run in tandem. In one, the central character manages to catch the train home on time and in the other she misses it. The two lives go in very different directions.

Genesis 4 contrasts the choices and consequences of two family lines in a similar way. The course of Cain's line was set when he 'went out from the Lord's presence' (v. 16). Whereas the Lord had ascribed to him the life of a nomad (v. 12), we find him establishing a city (v. 17)! By the seventh generation of Cain's line, we find Lamech introducing polygamy, boasting of murder and a blasphemous immunity to its consequences.

In contrast, Seth is portrayed as a substitute for Abel, a new shoot developing into the line that produces Jesus (Luke 3:23–38). The seventh son of his line was Enoch, who 'did not experience death' and 'was commended as one who pleased God' (Hebrews 11:5). It is in Seth's day that 'men began to call on the name of the Lord' (v. 26 above).

The contrasting lineages of Cain and Seth highlight a fundamental truth: humans have free will and can make genuine choices. That is why Solomon's advice is crucial: 'Trust in the Lord with all your heart and lean not on your own understanding; in all your ways acknowledge him, and he will make your paths straight' (Proverbs 3:5–6).

Prayer

Lord, in all my conscious decisions, please guide me. In all my unwitting choices, may your will be done. Amen

SA

Thirty sayings of the wise

We live, apparently, in the age of information. Enter a term in the Google search engine and you will discover more facts than you ever dreamed could exist—many of them completely irrelevant to your original enquiry, though still fascinating. I gather that TV presenter Jeremy Clarkson has said, 'There are a trillion facts on the internet, and every one of them is wrong.' Well, it may not be quite that bad, but it is true that more information does not necessarily equal more understanding.

The book of Proverbs belongs to the class of biblical writing known as 'Wisdom literature'. Especially in the three chapters we are going to look at in the next two weeks, it bears strong parallels with collections of sayings made by other Middle Eastern cultures of the time.

What is 'wisdom' in a biblical context? It is certainly not scientific knowledge, of which the writers had very little. Nor is it knowledge for its own sake, like a TV trivia quiz. Wisdom and folly, the major themes of Proverbs, are both words referring to things that we do, ways of living, rather than just intellectual speculation. Wisdom is to be practised, not just heard and forgotten.

If you remember the Radio 4 panel game *My Word*, you may know that the panellists were once called on to provide completely useless proverbs. The one that sticks in my mind is, 'No leg is too short to reach the ground' (which isn't even true, though it sounds vaguely profound)! Unlike these, the 'thirty sayings of the wise' (NIV) were written to be useful in everyday living. Ranging over the whole of human experience, they set out different choices, different paths in life, and predict their consequences. Addressed mainly to a hypothetical 'young man', by an older and wiser father figure, these proverbs can easily be applied to a wider range of readers and a different culture. Working honestly, making true friends, caring for the needy, avoiding temptation—these are goals that never go out of date.

Proverbs is not equivalent to the ministrations of a 'life coach', however. The difference between these sayings and their pagan parallels is that they describe a life lived in the view of the one God, who loves us and desires the best for us, and it is only through God's Spirit in us that we can take this ancient advice and live by it daily.

Veronica Zundel

Do talk to me about life

The words of the wise: Incline your ear and hear my words, and apply your mind to my teaching; for it will be pleasant if you keep them within you, if all of them are ready on your lips. So that your trust may be in the Lord, I have made them known to you today—yes, to you. Have I not written for you thirty sayings of admonition and knowledge, to show you what is right and true, so that you may give a true answer to those who sent you?

In my church the other Sunday, the theme for the worship and sermon was 'The Meaning of Life'. After some Monty Python quotes, the leader asked us three questions: 'What and from whom is the best piece of advice you have had about life?', 'What advice would you want to give about life?' and 'What does the Christian faith have to offer with regard to the meaning of life?'

I found the first two very hard to answer—perhaps I'm not very good at either accepting or giving advice! For the third, though, I wrote: 'A path to follow and someone to walk it with me.' It strikes me that the introductory paragraph that is our passage today is saying much the same thing: here is a way to live—'what is right and true'—and it is to be lived in the presence of God, 'so that your trust may be in the Lord'.

Proverbs is not a set of rules to adhere to, although it may sometimes look like one. It is more a set of attitudes and choices. Equally, the sayings are not meant to make our lives narrow and miserable. On the contrary, 'it will be pleasant if you keep them within you'.

On an Internet discussion board I run, one of our few rules is 'don't give advice unless it's asked for'. It seems it was asked for here: a group has sent a representative to ask for wisdom. Although this guidance on life is addressed to the individual—'yes, to you'—it is also to be shared, to be 'ready on your lips'. How often do we ask those older and wiser than us to give us advice on life? We might be surprised if we were to only ask them.

Prayer
'Give your servant therefore an understanding mind... able to discern between good and evil' (Solomon's prayer, 1 Kings 3:9).

VZ

The haves and have nots

> Do not rob the poor because they are poor, or crush the afflicted
> at the gate; for the Lord pleads their cause and despoils of life
> those who despoil them... Do not remove an ancient landmark or
> encroach on the fields of orphans, for their redeemer is strong; he
> will plead their cause against you.

Activist Jim Wallis once cut all references to the poor and needy out of
his Bible and held it up in a talk. It was literally in shreds, so constant
is this theme in God's word to us.

God is on the side of the poor. The argument of 'the wise' here is
that it is not just a poor person or family against whom you are offend-
ing if you exploit them, but God himself. As the king in Jesus' parable
says, 'Just as you did it to one of the least of these who are members of
my family, you did it to me' (Matthew 25:40). It's not surprising that
Proverbs appears to have been one of Jesus' favourite books of scripture.
Perhaps sayings like these inspired him to focus on the poor and needy.

Both the injunctions in the passage are about not exploiting your
neighbour: in those days, the only reason to move a landmark was to
annexe some of a neighbour's land. Land was the basis of the whole
economy, so to lose land was to lose your living. 'At the gate' was the
place where community leaders settled disputes, so those responsible
for applying the law are included here, too: the justice system should
not favour the wealthy.

Unfortunately for us in the affluent West, we are caught up in a system where some become rich at the expense of others. In order to stop
'robbing the poor', we may have to give up some aspects of our comfortable lifestyle that depend on their cheap labour and raw materials.

It is very difficult, perhaps impossible, to disentangle ourselves completely from economic injustice, but we can all make ourselves more
aware of its realities and speak out for a more just world. There are
many ways, some very simple, in which we can contribute to creating a
society that prioritises the poor and calls the wealthy to account.

Reflection

Does your church encourage you to think about economic inequalities?

VZ

Good and bad company

> Make no friends with those given to anger, and do not associate
> with hotheads, or you may learn their ways and entangle yourself
> in a snare... Do not speak in the hearing of a fool, who will only
> despise the wisdom of your words... Apply your mind to instruction
> and your ear to words of knowledge.

Gang-based shootings and stabbings in our inner cities are a chilling
reminder of how our actions are influenced by the company we keep.
It is perhaps understandable, given the level of deprivation in some
areas, that the young are angry with a society that has left them on the
scrapheap. Without the solidarity gangs provide, though, would they so
readily resort to violence?

As human beings we are inevitably influenced by those around us.
We live as part of a culture, sometimes of several overlapping cultures,
and our own families each have their own 'micro-culture'. For each of
us there will be assumptions and habits we never question—until we
come up against someone who does things differently. That is why our
churches need to be places of what a Mennonite leader calls 're-reflex-
ing'—the process whereby our automatic reactions are reprogrammed
to what God wants by spending time with others who live God's way.

2 Corinthians 6:17 exhorts us to be 'separate from them'. Christians
have often taken this to mean that we should live in a 'bubble' of our
Christian brothers and sisters, venturing out among the 'heathen' only
to evangelise them. I don't think that was Jesus' way. Indeed, he was
frequently in trouble for spending too much time with 'sinners' and he
prayed for his disciples, saying, 'I am not asking you to take them out of
the world, but I ask you to protect them from the evil one' (John 17:15).

As 'salt and light', Christians need to be both gathered and scattered:
gathered to gain strength in our values and attitudes and scattered to
influence our world. Each of us needs to find the right balance between
these two environments, so that our characters are shaped by good and
we have opportunities to practise that good among those who need it.

Reflection
Is your church a training ground for Christlikeness?

VZ

An honest day's work

> Do not be one of those who give pledges, who become surety for debts. If you have nothing with which to pay, why should your bed be taken from under you?... Do you see those who are skilful in their work? They will serve kings; they will not serve common people.

There's a frightening appropriateness, in a 'credit crunch' situation, about the first two verses of today's passage. They might at first look like a caution against generosity, but standing surety for a debt you cannot pay is not generosity; it's foolishness. We are instructed by the Bible to give generously, but not to lend stupidly.

I've put this thought together with verse 29 because it praises those who are conscientious in their work. Rather than working to make money, it suggests that the godly person is someone who works to make useful or beautiful things for others to enjoy. If we do our work well, who knows who our customers might be? Perhaps our product would even get one of those badges that say 'By Royal Appointment'.

Our global economy has increasingly become based on making money rather than on making goods. We even talk about 'financial products', as though a savings bond was something we can use around the house. We all need to make a living, but these verses suggest that pride in the quality of our work is just as important as how much we 'make' from it. Turning a fast buck is not promoted by the writers of Proverbs!

Even in a recession, 'What do you do?' is still the first question we tend to ask at parties. As Christians we know that, ultimately, we are defined by God's love for us rather than by our work, but *how* we do our work still speaks volumes about our character. The Victorian servant Hannah Cullwick wrote a detailed diary of her grinding, dirty daily work. She valued it, though, because she was doing it for the gentleman she had secretly married. Knowing that we work in the sight of God can make even drudgery a source of satisfaction.

Prayer
Teach me, my God and King, in all things Thee to see,
And what I do in anything, to do it as for Thee.

George Herbert, 1633
VZ

Who's coming to dinner?

When you sit down to eat with a ruler, observe carefully what is before you, and put a knife to your throat if you have a big appetite. Do not desire the ruler's delicacies, for they are deceptive food... Do not eat the bread of the stingy; do not desire their delicacies; for like a hair in the throat, so are they. 'Eat and drink!' they say to you; but they do not mean it. You will vomit up the little you have eaten, and you will waste your pleasant words.

I've never eaten with a ruler, I always use a fork! There, that's the bad joke out of the way. We move today from working for a king to eating with a king: perhaps the latter is a consequence of the former.

A huge amount of the Old Testament, and a surprising proportion of the New, is about food. Dietary customs were at the heart of Jewish religion, and what you ate and with whom were key to obedience to God. Feasts were the backbone of religious observance, which was based far more on the home than on the temple (giving women a vital role in ensuring that they were celebrated correctly).

Restraining one's greed when eating with royalty is just common sense, but this is joined by the advice not to yearn for posh dinners with celebrities: mixing with the famous can be a double-edged sword. In the 1930s my mother's cousin, an Austrian Jew, was a successful cabaret performer with his 'clairvoyant' act. Strangely, he found himself in favour with the top brass in the German Nazi party and was summoned to tell Hitler's fortune. When Hitler didn't like the result, he had the fortune teller shot and his body dumped in a field.

Of course, eating with the mean-minded is not much better. There is no pleasure in eating a meal, however good, with someone who has invited you out of duty. The upshot is: be selective about who you eat with and how. When we go to the Gospels, however, we find Jesus constantly in trouble for eating with the 'wrong' people. God's table has been opened wide in Christ and everyone is invited.

Reflection

'Then people will come from east and west, from north and south, and will eat in the kingdom of God' (Luke 13:29).

VZ

The green-eyed monster

Do not wear yourself out to get rich; be wise enough to desist. When your eyes light upon it, it is gone; for suddenly it takes wings to itself, flying like an eagle toward heaven... Do not let your heart envy sinners, but always continue in the fear of the Lord. Surely there is a future, and your hope will not be cut off... Do not envy the wicked, nor desire to be with them; for their minds devise violence, and their lips talk of mischief.

You know those moments when you're reading the Bible and it suddenly turns round and reads *you*? This is one of those moments for me. Envy is my besetting sin. The other day, I was sitting alone in a trendy new café where the 'yummy mummies' of North London gather. As I looked around, everyone was in pairs or groups, some with small children, and they all looked affluent and happy. At the next table, a woman of about my age was talking to her friend about the trip she was about to make to the Far East. I suddenly felt poor, friendless and underprivileged in comparison—even though I am actually none of those things!

It's easy to speculate about what my life might have been without chronic depression and imagine that others have marvellous, trouble-free lives, but, in reality, disaster can strike anyone at any time. A few years ago I met a college friend who seemed to have it all: two careers, a happy marriage, two grown-up kids, a slim figure and lovely tan, plus a house in France to boot. The next time I saw her, though, her 22-year-old daughter had been killed in a car crash.

There is a saying: 'The rich are different: they have more money'. Really, that's the only difference. A beautiful house or two, expensive possessions, skiing holidays and a place in the sun—all this is absolutely no guarantee that your life won't be turned upside down.

Putting our hope in God is not a guarantee against trouble, either, but it *is* a guarantee that our lives will ultimately have meaning and purpose and that death is no longer the great enemy.

Reflection

'The life I now live in the flesh I live by faith in the Son of God'
(Galatians 2:20).

VZ

Sparing the rod

Do not withhold discipline from your children; if you beat them with a rod, they will not die. If you beat them with the rod, you will save their lives from Sheol. My child, if your heart is wise, my heart too will be glad. My soul will rejoice when your lips speak what is right.

Recently my husband and I attended the annual review meeting of our son's statement of special needs. After years of battling with the education system, I was amazed to find that his subject teachers had all given him glowing reports. Pride in one's children's achievements is surely one of the least culpable sorts of pride!

The wise person here confidently expects to be able to take pride in a pupil's good character. I'm not a teacher but, as a parent, I still often experience the joy of watching a child learn something new.

What are we to make of that much-used, and often abused, injunction not to 'spare the rod'? Some Christians—I believe wrongly—interpret this to mean that Christian parents must use physical punishment. In fact, I think it's right that our society has moved away from the cane and the slipper. Hitting a child, however it is done, is essentially exercising power over a weaker person, so is contrary to the spirit of Jesus' teaching. Having said this, we've probably all 'lost it' at some time with our children and harsh words can be as hurtful as a blow. Love and forgiveness can heal many mistakes.

Personally, I would now do my utmost to avoid smacking my child (also, he's now bigger than me!) Does that mean that we don't discipline him? Far from it. I think we can take the spirit of this verse and say that disciplining children is essential, but it doesn't have to be physical. Children will only learn to set aside their immediate feelings and reason things out if adults give them an example of doing so.

Just a thought: sometimes people justify corporal punishment of children by saying 'It's the only language they understand'. If that's the case, why not teach them a better one? After all, isn't teaching us better ways to respond exactly what God is doing with us, his disciples?

Reflection

'The Lord disciplines those whom he loves' (Hebrews 12:6).

VZ

PROVERBS 23:20–21, 29–30, 33–35 (NRSV)

The demon drink

Do not be among winebibbers, or among gluttonous eaters of meat; for the drunkard and the glutton will come to poverty, and drowsiness will clothe them with rags... Who has woe? Who has sorrow? Who has strife? Who has complaining? Who has wounds without cause? Who has redness of eyes? Those who linger late over wine, those who keep trying mixed wines... Your eyes will see strange things, and your mind utter perverse things. You will be like one who lies down in the midst of the sea, like one who lies on the top of a mast. 'They struck me,' you will say, 'but I was not hurt; they beat me, but I did not feel it. When shall I awake? I will seek another drink.'

I've chosen a rather longer passage today, just because I love the vivid description here of being 'three sheets to the wind'. We may laugh at comic portrayals of drunks, but those who've lived with an alcoholic know that it's no laughing matter.

I dislike the sensation of being out of control, light-headed and nauseous, so I find it hard to understand people deliberately setting out to get so drunk that they are helpless. In Britain particularly, 'binge drinking' is a serious social problem. Thank God that there are Christian individuals and organisations who don't just warn against drink but also provide alternative entertainment for young people. We need more, though, as well as help for people suffering from the illness of alcoholism.

It's understandable that many Christians, seeing the damage that alcohol does to drinkers and their families, choose to abstain from it altogether. I'm not one of them: I believe that the Bible allows sensible use of alcohol. There are, however, multiple warnings in the scriptures against 'strong drink' (perhaps equivalent to our spirits).

Notice that greed for food is in the frame here, too. Eating disorders are also increasingly common. It seems that something has gone very wrong with our appetites. God gave us food and drink as good gifts; we need to pray for those who experience them only as a battleground.

Prayer
Giver of good gifts, heal those who struggle with food or drink
and bless those who work with them.

VZ

Make your parents proud

Listen to your father who begot you, and do not despise your mother when she is old. Buy truth, and do not sell it; buy wisdom, instruction, and understanding. The father of the righteous will greatly rejoice; he who begets a wise son will be glad in him. Let your father and mother be glad; let her who bore you rejoice.

It's fashionable to say that old people used to be at the heart of the family and command respect, unlike today when we put them in homes. It seems it isn't as simple as that: even at the time when these 'sayings of the wise' were collected, adult children needed to be reminded to honour their parents! We all lose some of our mental sharpness as we age, and the resulting slowness can be irritating to others. Not to mention grandparents' child-rearing advice, which is often less than welcome…

Jesus had, at best, an ambivalent attitude to his birth family: 'Who is my mother, and who are my brothers?… Whoever does the will of my Father in heaven is my brother and sister and mother' (Matthew 12:48–49). I'm not entirely surprised that he sometimes distanced himself from his family, given that they seem to have thought he was mad! Yet, even while he was dying on the cross, he made provision for his mother (John 19:26–27) and so united his biological and faith families. He was also scathing about those who put their religion before their dependants (Mark 7:10–13).

My mother was born in 1915 to a destitute refugee, was immediately fostered, then later adopted. She regards her adoptive parents as her 'real' parents; after all, they were the ones who brought her up. She and her mother didn't always get on, but my childhood was still peppered with quotes from my grandmother. Sadly my mother was unable to rescue her from death in a concentration camp, at the age of only 61.

Elderly parents may sometimes feel like a burden, but, in fact, it is a privilege to still have them. I know my friends who lost their parents early would love to have them back.

Reflection

'I bow my knees before the Father, from whom every family in heaven and on earth takes its name' (Ephesians 3:14–15).

VZ

The tender trap

> My child, give me your heart, and let your eyes observe my ways.
> For a prostitute is a deep pit; an adulteress is a narrow well. She
> lies in wait like a robber and increases the number of the faithless.

What is it about being a Christian leader or, indeed, a political leader, that seems so to dispose people to sexual transgression? Time and again we hear of a preacher or cabinet minister having to resign because of a sex scandal. Of course, ordinary people fall into such traps, too—they just get less publicity. Blaming the woman involved—'She threw herself at me'—is no escape.

Proverbs sometimes comes perilously close to putting all the blame on women for promiscuity and adultery. Ultimately, though, it holds men to be just as responsible: men are challenged to take responsibility for their own sexual desires, not portray themselves as helpless victims. So, among the many kinds of advice given to the young man who is addressed in Proverbs, 'the wise' warn against sexual misconduct. They don't, however, make the mistake common among many Christians of rating sexual sins as more serious than any other kind. Sex is just one of the many different temptations that can lure the disciple.

The Bible tells us that Jesus faced every kind of temptation that we do (Hebrews 4:15). There were many women, travelling without their husbands, who followed him. He expected his male disciples, and himself, to relate to them as people, though, not sex objects.

I once heard an agony aunt on the radio say that you can't argue with teenage hormones. I thought that was dangerous nonsense, practically justifying rape. The hormones are, after all, part of a person and you can argue with a person. Although the verses here are addressed to a young man, this warning is just as applicable to women—of any age!

I find it interesting that sexual sin is described as 'increas[ing] the number of the faithless'. Faith often founders on the rocks of wayward desire. The remedy is, rather than gazing at the person you wrongly desire, to 'let your eyes observe' your mentors and role models.

Reflection
'My child, give me your heart.'

VZ

Peacebuilding

By wisdom a house is built, and by understanding it is established; by knowledge the rooms are filled with all precious and pleasant riches. Wise warriors are mightier than strong ones, and those who have knowledge than those who have strength; for by wise guidance you can wage your war, and in abundance of counsellors there is victory.

This reminds me of Jesus' parable about the houses built on sand and on rock (Matthew 7:24–27). We know, from many parallels, that Proverbs was one of Jesus' favourite books, but we also know that it's not bricklaying techniques that are under discussion here. 'A house' means a household of people, related or unrelated, who live together. The 'precious and pleasant riches' are not just art objects, but qualities such as patience, generosity and helpfulness that enable people to live together in peace. Getting on with those closest to us may be the hardest work we ever do and it requires more wisdom than any other.

What do we do when our wisdom fails and two communities—perhaps two nations or ethnic groups—can no longer manage to live in peace with each other? Can we fight wars with the wisdom of God? Those who have fought wars would surely testify that wisdom in strategy is just as important as having the latest equipment. Throughout the Old Testament (for instance, in Joshua), there is testimony that it is God's will, not superior weaponry, that wins battles.

As a Christian pacifist, however, I believe that, in Christ, we are under a new covenant where to kill, even for 'good' causes, is no longer acceptable. Christ teaches us to love our enemies and pray for persecutors and he died an unjust death without fighting back. One peace organisation has a poster with a simple proposal: that the Christians of the world agree not to kill each other. Is that too much to ask?

Do we apply the same thought, effort and resources to peacemaking as we do to winning wars? If the same amount of funds and the same number of people were deployed in conflict resolution, we might be amazed at how much more peaceful the world could become.

Prayer
Prince of Peace, make us peacemakers.

VZ

PROVERBS 24:8–9, 15–16 (NRSV)

Crime and punishment

Whoever plans to do evil will be called a mischief-maker. The devising of folly is sin, and the scoffer is an abomination to all... Do not lie in wait like an outlaw against the home of the righteous; do no violence to the place where the righteous live; for though they fall seven times, they will rise again; but the wicked are overthrown by calamity.

What is 'the devising of folly'? 'Folly' here does not mean silly jokes; it is an action word, just as 'wisdom' is. Both folly and wisdom appear not only in what we think or say but also in what we do. In fact, you can't find out if people are really wise unless you see something of their lives.

Here, 'the wise' do some straight talking about the roots of crime. Most crime is not, as newspapers routinely describe it, 'mindless'. As much ingenuity, boldness and determination can be shown in the committing of a crime as in everyday work. It's just that these qualities are directed to the wrong ends. Occasionally a violent criminal has been turned around by the guidance or education they have been given in prison and proven to be a talented, dynamic person whose abilities can now be used constructively. Sadly, our prison system is largely punitive rather than reforming and such cases are rare.

I have a confession. One of my favourite female characters in the Bible is Jezebel. Yes, I know she was scheming, greedy and contemptuous of God's prophets, but what a powerful personality she had and what a superb asset she could have been on God's side! Her story is an illustration of the truth in today's sayings. Poverty, a broken-down culture, lack of opportunity—all are factors in the genesis of crime. No crime can happen, however, unless a person's will is being directed towards it.

It's too easy for us just to 'tut' over crime. Even 'the righteous'—those who love God—will fall continually. Perhaps this is one of the many ways in which we can be like a 'little child', as Jesus put it (Mark 10:15), who, when they fall, cry a bit, then pick themselves up and, within a few minutes, are following Dad or Mum and smiling again.

Prayer
'You desire truth in the inward being; therefore teach me wisdom in my secret heart' (Psalm 51:6).

VZ

When life hurts

If you faint in the day of adversity, your strength being small; if you hold back from rescuing those taken away to death, those who go staggering to the slaughter; if you say, 'Look, we did not know this'—does not he who weighs the heart perceive it? Does not he who keeps watch over your soul know it? And will he not repay all according to their deeds?

In his book *God on Mute* (Regal, 2007), Pete Greig suggests that, if we are to make sense of our unanswered prayers, we need 'a theology of suffering'. Trying to convince yourself that every request will be granted and every sick person healed is putting your own head in the sand and misleading others. After all, if we could set the whole world right just by saying a few prayers, we'd virtually be God ourselves, wouldn't we?

Suffering is part of life in a fallen world; why should Christians be excused? In my home congregation, in the last few years we have had several distressing deaths—most recently the death from cancer of a 20-year-old girl whose father also died from the same condition. Now her mother has incurable cancer. Yet, that same mother's faith remains strong and she continues to serve others.

We may accept suffering for ourselves, but how should we respond to the suffering of others? Proverbs tells us that our calling is to take note when others are unjustly imprisoned or executed, to make it our business to be aware of the world's needs and respond to them as best we can. 'I didn't know' is no excuse—certainly not in our world of mass communication. That's the trouble, though: we know so much about the suffering in this world, the hunger, oppression, torture. Where do we begin to try to alleviate it? What can one person do?

I don't think God expects everyone to be doing everything. Perhaps, though, God does expect everyone to be doing something. Each of us—and, on a larger scale, the Church together—is called by God to care for the suffering in some way, whether it's by giving money, actively volunteering or making others aware of their needs.

Reflection
'Show me your faith without works, and I by my works will show you my faith' (James 2:18).

VZ

No revenge fantasies

> Do not rejoice when your enemies fall, and do not let your heart be glad when they stumble, or else the Lord will see it and be displeased, and turn away his anger from them. Do not fret because of evildoers. Do not envy the wicked; for the evil have no future; the lamp of the wicked will go out.

The German language has a word, sometimes used in English: *Schadenfreude*. It means taking pleasure in the misfortune of others. That is the subject for today.

One of my favourite psalms is Psalm 73. As I said earlier, envy is my biggest weakness and the writer of that psalm is seething with envy of 'the wicked': 'their bodies are sound and sleek. They are not in trouble as others are; they are not plagued like other people' (vv. 4–5). It seems that good things happen to bad people, while the people of God endure trial after trial. 'My feet had almost stumbled', says the psalmist, until he went to the temple to seek God and then, 'I perceived their end' (vv. 2, 17). It is a theme that is repeated in the Old Testament: while the ungodly may appear to prosper, in the final reckoning they will come to nothing, they will be blown away like husks (Psalm 1:4).

Here in Proverbs, though, there's an extra instruction: we are not to enjoy the downfall of those who have hurt us. We must remember that God loves our enemies just as much as he loves us, and if God was not an enemy-lover, where would we be?

Jesus goes even further: 'Do not resist an evildoer' (Matthew 5:39). This does not mean that we should be passive in the face of evil, but we should not use the evildoer's own weapons—anger, vindictive words, violence—against their evil. Instead, we should 'put on the whole armour of God' (Ephesians 6:11). What are God's weapons? Love, faithfulness, forgiveness, the word of truth, the promise of peace. Only these can truly disarm the armies of injustice, greed and hatred.

Reflection

'If we do not think it possible to love our enemies then we should plainly say that Jesus is not the messiah' (Stanley Hauerwas). Does this apply on a political level as well as a personal one?

VZ

Sweet honey from the rock

My child, eat honey, for it is good, and the drippings of the honeycomb are sweet to your taste. Know that wisdom is such to your
soul; if you find it, you will find a future, and your hope will not be
cut off... My child, fear the Lord and the king, and do not disobey
either of them; for disaster comes from them suddenly, and who
knows the ruin that both can bring?

My father was something of a connoisseur of honey and was convinced
that eating it regularly would make him live longer, especially if he
ate the honeycomb, too. For people living in the times and places of
the Bible, honey was dangerous and difficult to obtain and the only
sweetener they had. There was none of the added sugar we have in our
processed foods, so it was a real treat.

We are used to the idea of the Bible as 'daily bread', our staple
spiritual diet, but this passage suggests that it is also a food for special
days and feasts. I have a sweet tooth, but sometimes just a mouthful
of something sweet is enough to keep me going. Likewise, sometimes
a single verse of the Bible comes to my mind and sustains me in the
midst of troubles.

I think the book of Proverbs works that way: each pithy saying is fuel
for a great deal of thought and can build character. Perhaps one or two a
day would be the recommended daily amount! Through regular reading
and hearing— of not only scripture but also other people's thoughts on
it—we can build up a store of God's word and have it ready to give us
sustenance when we are faced with a difficult decision or a crisis.

I don't think this is saying that the Bible will have an easy answer
for every question we ask. It's not Wikipedia! Being 'well fed' with the
Bible, however, can make us into the kinds of people God needs for the
kingdom—as long as we don't use it to promote our personal or political ends. As for 'fear the king', we are to respect governments, but there
will always be times when 'We must obey God rather than any human
authority' (Acts 5:29). God's wisdom can tell us when those times are.

Prayer
'Teach me to do your will, for you are my God' (Psalm 143:10).

VZ

Ignatius of Loyola

What connects Inigo Lopez—an obscure Spanish soldier, born in 1491, the son of an aristocratic family in a remote Basque village—to Ignatius Loyola, a saint and spiritual guide to many 21st-century pilgrims in search of a deeper relationship with God?

The answer makes rather interesting reading. The story is of how a proud, ambitious and self-willed young man was brought to his knees, literally and spiritually, in battle and experienced a dramatic conversion. It transformed him into the founder of what would eventually become one of the largest religious orders in the Roman Catholic Church—the Society of Jesus, also known as the Jesuits. It is also a story of a pilgrim's journey through the heights of religious experience and the depths of self-doubt as he confronted his demons. It reveals how our reflections on our own everyday experience can be pointers to the deeper inner movements of our souls.

Ignatius explored most of his formative experience while he was a layperson and so, in the earlier of these reflections, we will call him Inigo. When he tried to spread the word that God can be met in the everyday world, always seeking to guide our choices and actions into the most life-giving ways, he met opposition from the Church of the time because it could not countenance the possibility that an untutored layman could be preaching God's word. As a result, he set himself the task of learning Latin, studying theology, too, and eventually he was ordained as a priest. At that point, he took the name Ignatius so that he could more freely pursue his mission.

Today, Ignatian spirituality is welcomed by countless contemporary spiritual pilgrims as a way of deepening prayer using scriptural meditation, reflective awareness and the tools of spiritual discernment to make wiser choices in our daily lives. During the next two weeks leading up to the feast of Ignatius on 31 July, we will explore some of the ways in which his story resonates with our own stories.

The prayer of Richard of Chichester, often associated with Ignatius, sums him up very succinctly. His desire for Christ was always 'to see you more clearly, love you more dearly, follow you more nearly, day by day.' The legacy Ignatius has left us can help us to do the same.

Margaret Silf

2 Corinthians 12:7b–10 (NRSV)

Laid low

Therefore, to keep me from being too elated, a thorn was given to me in the flesh, a messenger from Satan to torment me, to keep me from being too elated. Three times I appealed to the Lord about this, that it would leave me, but he said to me, 'My grace is sufficient for you, for power is made perfect in weakness.' So, I will boast all the more gladly of my weaknesses, so that the power of Christ may dwell in me. Therefore I am content with weaknesses, insults, hardships, persecutions, and calamities for the sake of Christ; for whenever I am weak, then I am strong.

It may surprise you to learn that you are only reading this because of a stray cannon ball that hit a young Spanish soldier in the knee during a long-forgotten battle between the Spanish and the French in northern Spain. That soldier's name was Inigo, youngest son of a family of 13 and a nobleman-in-training.

He was a proud young man, rather hot-headed, with ambitions for a glorious military career and an eye for the ladies. It was while defending an indefensible position at the fortress of Pamplona that he received his own version of Paul's 'thorn'. His knee was shattered by the said cannon ball and he had to be carried home on a stretcher to the family castle at Loyola, where he was to spend many long months recuperating and reflecting on how he really wanted his life to be.

How often does it happen that only when we are 'laid low', perhaps by illness or accident or some disappointment or loss, do we go deeper and discover new perspectives on what life means for us and even who God is for us. A story is told about a tribe of people who spent their lives searching for a holy mountain. One day, one of them fell over as the tribe hurried on their way and, as he lay on the ground, helpless, he looked up and there it was: the holy mountain. Some things we only see when we are reduced to helplessness.

Reflection

Have you had the experience of being 'laid low'? With hindsight, did that experience draw you closer to God and to other people? Did it in any way help to show how God's power is revealed most effectively in our weakness?

MS

GENESIS 41:1–7 (NRSV)

Dreaming

After two whole years, Pharaoh dreamed that he was standing by the Nile, and there came up out of the Nile seven sleek and fat cows, and they grazed in the reed grass. Then seven other cows, ugly and thin, came up out of the Nile after them, and stood by the other cows on the bank of the Nile. The ugly and thin cows ate up the seven sleek and fat cows. And Pharaoh awoke. Then he fell asleep and dreamed a second time; seven ears of grain, plump and good, were growing on one stalk. Then seven ears, thin and blighted by the east wind, sprouted after them. The thin ears swallowed up the seven plump and full ears. Pharaoh awoke, and it was a dream.

Inigo wasn't the easiest of patients. The cannon ball had not only shot through his knee but also his dreams and made a rather big hole in his ego, too. A bored convalescent, he eventually asked for some books to read and was given two: the *Life of Christ* and the *Lives of the Saints*. His comments on being offered this selection of light reading, mercifully, were not recorded.

Desperation, though, can sometimes be God's best ally. In between periods of reading, Inigo indulged in a spot of daydreaming—first about his old fantasies of fame and fortune and then, in contrast, 'out-sainting the saints'. If Francis and Dominic and Benedict could do these amazing things for God, surely he could do even greater things. As you can see, humility hadn't yet caught up with him.

Then, however, he began to notice a strange difference between his 'worldly' dreams and his 'saintly' dreams. The former left him feeling flat and low and discontented, while the latter left him feeling keyed up and energised, eager to become more like the saints he was reading about, the Christ he was encountering through their stories. This was the beginning of his conversion. God was on his heels and the dreaming was to prove crucial in all that lay ahead.

Reflection

Take time to reflect on the day or week just gone. What has made you feel more alive, more energised? What has left you feeling flat and low? Think about whether God is trying to show you something in these reactions.

MS

Choosing what leads to life

[Jesus said to his disciples] 'Do not work for the food that per-
ishes, but for the food that endures for eternal life, which the Son
of Man will give you. For it is on him that God the Father has set
his seal... Very truly, I tell you, it was not Moses who gave you
the bread from heaven, but it is my Father who gives you the true
bread from heaven. For the bread of God is that which comes
down from heaven and gives life to the world. They said to him,
'Sir, give us this bread always.' Jesus said to them, 'I am the bread
of life. Whoever comes to me will never be hungry, and whoever
believes in me will never be thirsty.'

In his own way, Inigo was discovering the truth of these words. He
was beginning to realise that so far in his life he had been putting all
his energy into the pursuit of fame and glory. What had it led him to?
A sickbed in a remote backwater where he felt like a nobody. He
couldn't even cut a fine figure in the ballroom any more. Such was his
pride that he went through the agony of having his leg broken again and
reset because the first attempt had left one leg shorter than the other.

His daydreams about worldly glory were showing him how empty
the world's promises really are when everything that he had valued
could be shattered in a moment and reduced to pain and regret. His
daydreams about following the example of the saints, however, were
showing him that there is a kind of life-bread that truly satisfies. There
is another way. In his mind and heart Inigo was grappling with some
of the key questions that spiritual pilgrims ask. What parts of my life
are to do with becoming more fully alive, more fully the person God is
dreaming me to be and what parts of my life are perishable, like cake
that tastes so good, but does not last? What is the real me about? Which
dreams do I actually desire to follow?

Reflection
*Think about your own deepest dreams. Which ones seem to you to have
their roots in God? Which dreams do you most want to follow?*

MS

The conqueror surrenders

The very night before Herod was going to bring him out, Peter, bound with two chains, was sleeping between two soldiers, while guards in front of the door were keeping watch over the prison. Suddenly an angel of the Lord appeared and a light shone in the cell. He tapped Peter on the side and woke him, saying 'Get up quickly.' And the chains fell off his wrists. The angel said to him, 'Fasten your belt and put on your sandals.' He did so. Then he said to him, 'Wrap your cloak around you and follow me.' Peter went out and followed him; he did not realise that what was happening with the angel's help was real; he thought he was seeing a vision.

Never a man to do things by halves, Inigo was to experience a dramatic conversion. Today the castle at Loyola has a chapel with a rather flamboyant statue of the incipient saint at the moment of his conversion.

God, as we have seen, had been preparing the ground. Like Peter, Inigo had been locked into a prison, but a prison of his own making: in chains of self-absorption, pride and overweening ambition, under the power of the illusion of not only self-sufficiency but also even indestructibility. The world, he had believed, was his to conquer and nothing, he thought, could stop him. In God's school of sainthood, however, Inigo was going to find himself right back in the beginners' class.

The stray cannon ball that struck him down was to break the first chain. The unconquerable commander became a helpless convalescent. Weakened and humbled, Inigo's heart was gradually being softened to allow God's power to break through, and break through it did.

So, there, in a room in the castle, Inigo surrendered to a higher power and made his choice to follow Jesus. From that moment on there would be no looking back. He declared his intention of following the Lord in the face of considerable opposition from his family. He determined to change his life completely, letting go all ambition, except for one dream—to follow Jesus more nearly, wherever that might lead him.

Reflection

Inigo's conversion was dramatic, but sometimes God calls gently and almost imperceptibly. How do you remember your own turning to God?

MS

Hands on the plough

As they were going along the road, someone said to [Jesus], 'I will follow you wherever you go.' And Jesus said to him, 'Foxes have holes, and birds of the air have nests; but the Son of Man has nowhere to lay his head.' To another he said, 'Follow me.' But he said, 'Lord, first let me go and bury my father.' But Jesus said to him, 'Let the dead bury their own dead; but as for you, go and proclaim the kingdom of God.' Another said, 'I will follow you, Lord; but let me first say farewell to those at my home.' Jesus said to him, 'No one who puts a hand to the plough and looks back is fit for the kingdom of God.'

Inigo may have had his shortcomings, but lack of commitment certainly wasn't one of them. Once he had put his hand to God's plough, there really was no looking back. He gave away his nobleman's clothes to a passing beggar as a sign that he meant business with regard to living simply. Unfortunately, the poor beggar was later arrested on suspicion of having stolen the clothes!

Leaving behind his dismayed family, Inigo set off on his pilgrimage for God, which was to be a lifetime's quest. Yet, still there was a good deal more Inigo than God in the equation. He had already decided where he was going. His destination was to be the Holy Land, where he would single-handedly convert the unbelievers. The conquering hero was still very much in control. In fact, as it would turn out, the particular doors that Inigo had in mind remained decisively closed to him. Both shipwreck and bureaucracy would conspire to prevent him from ever realising his dream to become God's servant in God's holy land. As the years passed, he would discover that commitment to God usually involves letting go of our own ideas of how things should go.

Even so, he was learning! He began his new life by making his way to the Abbey of Montserrat, to make his gesture of surrender to God and his confession—a confession that, we are told, lasted about three days.

Reflection

What does 'commitment' mean to you? Has your own pattern of
commitment changed through the years?

MS

Letting go of the defences

Owe no one anything, except to love one another; for the one who loves another has fulfilled the law... Beside this, you know what time it is, how it is now the moment for you to wake from sleep. For salvation is nearer to us now than when we became believers; the night is far gone, the day is near. Let us then lay aside the works of darkness and put on the armour of light; let us live honourably as in the day, not in revelling and drunkenness, not in debauchery and licentiousness, not in quarrelling and jealousy. Instead, put on the Lord Jesus Christ, and make no provision for the flesh, to gratify its desires.

The Abbey of Montserrat is perched high among the jagged precipices of a dramatic mountain ridge. It is home to the statue of the Black Madonna, which was where Inigo chose to carry out his own ritual of surrender. There he laid down his weapons, leaving his sword and dagger behind on the altar as a sign that he was now God's soldier, and his mule to the monks. So, he would have identified strongly with today's passage, recalling his own laying aside of the works of darkness and his vow to live honourably from then on as a humble servant of God.

From Montserrat he set forth, leaving behind a life of quarrels, wars and maybe even a little debauchery, making no provision for his earthly needs, but entrusting himself entirely—recklessly, some might say—to God's providence.

At a deeper level, perhaps, he was also setting aside his own defences. What defences do we carry with us? What might we need to surrender as we move forward on our journey with God? Defences and coping strategies can come in many different guises. For example, a reluctance to try something new in case we fail, a tendency to adopt a 'victim' role to evoke sympathy, or to push our own opinions and never listen to other people's views. The most aggressive people are often the most insecure. Their aggression is their armour against the exposure of weakness.

Reflection

Make your own prayer of surrender, naming before God those defences that you desire to leave behind as you walk forward in trust.

MS

Mountain high, valley deep

Jesus took with him Peter and John and James, and went up on the mountain to pray. And while he was praying, the appearance of his face changed, and his clothes became dazzling white. Suddenly they saw two men, Moses and Elijah, talking to him. They appeared in glory and were speaking of his departure, which he was about to accomplish at Jerusalem... On the next day, when they had come down from the mountain, a great crowd met him. Just then a man from the crowd shouted, 'Teacher, I beg you to look at my son; he is my only child. Suddenly a spirit seizes him, and all at once he shrieks. It throws him into convulsions until he foams at the mouth; it mauls him and will scarcely leave him. I begged your disciples to cast it out, but they could not.'

From the mountaintop of Montserrat, you can look down and imagine that you can see the entire continent of Europe spread out at your feet. For Inigo, it was both physically and spiritually a mountaintop experience. His conversion had led him to this high place, where he had made his surrender of mind, heart and will. He had been absolved of all that lay in the past and now he was ready for anything!

We have mountaintop experiences, too. For example, when we feel that we have come very close to God, maybe in prayer or during a retreat, or when something wonderful touches our hearts and we feel we are, spiritually, on top of the world. Today we encounter Jesus in just such a place, where the eternal reality of who he is totally transcends the physical limitations of his earthly life. Perhaps each of us knows, in our own much smaller way, something of how this can feel.

Inigo could be forgiven for thinking that this was it. That he had arrived and now all paths lay open before him. He was due for a big surprise because the thing about mountaintops is that you have to come down from them and at the bottom waits the real world—people begging for help, the sick, the poor, the desperate.

Reflection

The seed of a vision may be sown on the mountaintop, but the labour and the harvest happen in the valley.

MS

Facing the demons

I do not understand my own actions. For I do not do what I want,
but I do the very thing I hate. Now if I do what I do not want,
I agree that the law is good. But in fact it is no longer I that do it,
but sin that dwells within me. For I know that nothing good dwells
within me, that is, in my flesh. I can will what is right, but I cannot
do it. For I do not do the good I want, but the evil I do not want is
what I do. Now if I do what I do not want, it is no longer I that do
it, but sin that dwells within me. So I find it to be a law that when
I want to do what is good, evil lies close at hand.

Montserrat overlooks the plain of Manresa and it was to the town
of Manresa that Inigo made his way, intending to stay there for just
a few days until he could prepare for his journey to the Holy Land.
God, though, had other ideas! In the event, Inigo would spend eleven
months in Manresa and they would be life-changing months.

Today, Paul shares with us his problem of failing to do the good he
desires to do and doing the very thing he doesn't want to do. It's a
feeling that most of us can share. We look back over the day, and we
see so many times when, despite our high ideals, we failed miserably.
Scruples like this afflicted Inigo. He constantly saw himself as falling
short of God's expectations and even slipped into extreme and destructive asceticism and self-neglect.

Yet it was here, while ministering to the poorest of the poor, that he
began to discern the different movements stirring in his heart and recognise which were creative and from God and which were destructive
and not from God. As he grappled with his 'angels' and 'demons', he
was growing in a self-awareness that would help him to discern God's
guidance. He was also keeping notes that would later form his 'Spiritual
Exercises', which continue to help thousands of pilgrims today in their
journey with God.

Reflection

*Take some time to notice the movements in your heart through the
past day. Which were creative? Which were destructive?*

MS

Every choice counts

See, I have set before you today life and prosperity, death and adversity. If you obey the commandments of the Lord your God that I am commanding you today, by loving the Lord your God, walking in his ways, and observing his commandments, decrees, and ordinances, then you shall live and become numerous, and the Lord your God will bless you in the land that you are entering to possess... I call heaven and earth to witness against you today that I have set before you life and death, blessings and curses. Choose life so that you and your descendants may live, loving the Lord your God, obeying him, and holding fast to him.

Of course, simply being aware of the inner movements stirring in our hearts (which we were thinking about yesterday), important though that is, won't take us too far unless we are prepared to embrace the next step. That is to choose to follow the creative movements we sense and withdraw our attention from the destructive ones—or even, if necessary, actively work against them.

Inigo was soon to learn that the essence of following Jesus lies in our choices. Every choice we make, whether trivial or major, affects the whole of creation and either brings humanity a little closer to God's dream or tips it a little further away. Every choice either adds to the store of love, hope and trust in the world or diminishes it, however slightly. No choice is neutral.

So the question we face is, in a specific situation, what is the more loving thing to do next? Of course, not all choices are so black and white. Sometimes we will have to choose the least harmful way forward. Sometimes the choice will lie between the good and the better or the better and the best. God calls us always to seek the more loving, the more life-giving, the more Christlike way. Inigo was discovering this dynamic in his own life and he was given the grace to share the wisdom he gained in a process of prayer that has not only survived but also blossomed in the Christian Church for 500 years.

Reflection

The good can sometimes be the enemy of the better. May we always have the courage to choose the better way.

MS

MATTHEW 6:5–8 (NRSV)

Living reflectively

[Jesus said] 'And whenever you pray, do not be like the hypocrites; for they love to stand and pray in the synagogues and at the street corners, so that they may be seen by others. Truly I tell you, they have received their reward. But whenever you pray, go into your room and shut the door and pray to your Father who is in secret; and your Father who sees in secret will reward you. When you are praying, do not heap up empty phrases as the Gentiles do; for they think that they will be heard because of their many words. Do not be like them, for your Father knows what you need before you ask him.'

The approach to spirituality that has become known as 'Ignatian' is characterised, among other things, by its encouragement of some forms of prayer that many people find helpful and possibly new and unfamiliar. I can well remember how I was first introduced to these forms of prayer and what a breath of fresh air they brought. Ignatius (for now, perhaps, we should give him his full Latin name) did not invent these ways of prayer, but he strongly endorsed them. They have their roots in the earliest Christian traditions and have been used through the centuries by countless Christians seeking a closer walk with God.

Possibly the most important of them all is the prayer variously known as the 'Examen', or simply the 'Review of the Day'. This invites us to take time each day to look back over what has actually been going on in our lives and how we feel the movements of our heart to have been. Where was God in our day? What might we want to give thanks for? What might we need to express regret for? What has left us feeling more alive? How have our choices worked out during this day and how have they affected other people? Questions like these can bring us into a space of reflective awareness, where the events of our everyday lives can be seen from a deeper perspective.

Ignatius urged his companions to make time for this reflective prayer every day, even if they were too busy to do anything else.

Reflection
A drop of silence is worth a waterfall of words.

MS

Wednesday 28 July

MATTHEW 13:31–34 (NRSV)

Finding God in all things

[Jesus] put before them another parable: 'The kingdom of heaven
is like a mustard seed that someone took and sowed in his field;
it is the smallest of all the seeds, but when it has grown it is the
greatest of shrubs and becomes a tree, so that the birds of the
air come and make nests in its branches.' He told them another
parable: 'The kingdom of heaven is like yeast that a woman took
and mixed in with three measures of flour until all of it was leav-
ened.' Jesus told the crowds all these things in parables; without
a parable he told them nothing.

Today we see Jesus using the method he favoured most when teaching
people about the things of God. He chooses to direct his audience's
attention to something very ordinary in their everyday experience, then
he makes connections with the nature of God and God's kingdom. We
call this approach using parables and tend to think of them as something we find in the Bible, but actually parables are everywhere and we
can find them wherever we look, if we reflect on our experience.

This links to another characteristic of Ignatian spirituality: 'finding
God in all things'. It is what incarnational spirituality means: discovering the hand of God in the daily realities of human life. In fact, this
approach is at the heart of all Christian spirituality and it lies at the
heart of the Gospel, as we can see in today's passage.

One of the graces of praying the Review prayer is that we begin to
notice, more consciously, the parables in our own daily living. We start
to look out for the hand of God and ask for the grace to see it for ourselves, not just in ancient stories, but in our personal story.

Suppose someone were to say to you today: 'What is this God-stuff
all about? What is this kingdom?' How would you respond? I suggest
that doctrines and sermons might well not work with your enquirer,
but what about a parable? What can you find in your own real, lived
experience that shows you something about what God's reign is like?

Reflection

*Take a walk along your nearest high street and see if you can notice
the hand of God at work.*

MS

102

Immersing ourselves in the gospel

As [Jesus] was setting out on a journey, a man ran up to him and knelt before him, and asked him, 'Good Teacher, what must I do to inherit eternal life?' Jesus said to him, 'Why do you call me good? No one is good but God alone. You know the commandments: "You shall not murder; you shall not commit adultery; you shall not steal; you shall not bear false witness; you shall not defraud; honour your father and your mother."' He said to him, 'Teacher, I have kept all these since my youth.' Jesus, looking at him, loved him and said, 'You lack one thing; go, sell what you own, and give the money to the poor, and you will have treasure in heaven; then come, follow me.' When he heard this, he was shocked and went away grieving, for he had many possessions.

If God is in all things, then God is also indwelling in the depths of the human psyche. We move today to another feature of Ignatian spirituality: the invitation to allow our imaginations to be engaged when we pray.

We meet a young man who longs to come closer to God. He is a good, practising Jew, but he is clinging to stuff that will impede his journey. When we read this passage, the questions we are invited to ask by Ignatian spirituality are not so much, 'Who was this man?' or 'Did this really happen?', but, rather, 'What does this story mean?' and 'What might Jesus be saying to *me* through it?' We are invited to make our own connections. One way to do so is to try to imagine ourselves encountering Jesus personally, asking our own questions and then listening to Jesus' response. This form of prayer is known as imaginative meditation. If you have never tried it, you might like to do so.

How do we know that this is prayer, though, and not just daydreaming? Well, there are worse things to daydream about than Gospel stories, but if it is rooted in God, then, sooner or later, it will make a difference. It will change us or our attitudes in some way.

Reflection

Using this, or any other Gospel story, ask God to help you see what it means for you, now, in your own circumstances.

MS

Turning contemplation into action

[Jesus said to the chief priests and elders] 'What do you think?
A man had two sons; he went to the first and said, "Son, go and
work in the vineyard today." He answered, "I will not"; but later
he changed his mind and went. The father went to the second
and said the same; and he answered, "I go, sir"; but he did not
go. Which of the two did the will of his father?' They said, 'The
first.' Jesus said to them, 'Truly I tell you, the tax collectors and
the prostitutes are going into the kingdom of God ahead of you.'

Ignatius was always a man of action. His whole story was one of active
engagement with the world and he carried this passion for action into
his spiritual life after his conversion. In fact, it is a feature of Ignatian
spirituality to speak of 'turning contemplation into action'.

An image that helps me understand this is that of an oil lamp. The
lamp's wick has two ends. If the lamp is to burn, then one end of the
wick must be immersed in the oil and the other end must be extended
out into the world. If neither of these conditions is met, there will be
no light.

So it is in our own lives. We need to remain 'immersed in God',
through prayer and reflections, and at the same time be open and
available and active in the world in which we live. If we can do this, we
will be 'contemplatives in action', just as Jesus was, always ready and
energised to bring the light of the Gospel to bear on every choice and
action in our daily living.

Putting prayer into action isn't so hard: it simply means doing what
we know we have to do, having listened to the movements of God in
our hearts. Today's passage, though, reveals all too clearly that it isn't
always so easy. Too often we say 'Yes, yes' in our prayer, but then do
nothing about it, like the first son in Jesus' story. Jesus warns us that
God is better served by the second son, who first of all refused to do
what was asked of him, but later, having reflected, went and did it.

Reflection

How is your lamp: are both ends of the wick where they should be?

MS

1 JOHN 4:7–9, 11–12 (NRSV)

A little loving goes a long way

Beloved, let us love one another, because love is from God; every-one who loves is born of God and knows God. Whoever does not love does not know God, for God is love. God's love was revealed among us in this way: God sent his only Son into the world so that we might live through him... Beloved, since God loved us so much, we also ought to love one another. No one has ever seen God; if we love one another, God lives in us, and his love is perfected in us.

The Ignatian 'Spiritual Exercises' end with an invitation to reflect on how we might, in our own way, begin to learn to love others with the kind of love that God reveals. This means loving whether or not the 'other' appears lovable or we happen to feel like it, and even when there is no prospect of any kind of payback, any kind of reciprocation.

This kind of loving is a huge challenge and can only really come from God, yet we are asked to emulate it. It clearly can't depend on our emo-tions, but it can be revealed in our decisions. However we feel, we can choose to act in the more loving way.

I remember my first trip up the Empire State Building in New York City. It was dark and, when I looked down on the teeming city below, I was spellbound, it was so beautiful. Then it occurred to me that this wasn't some million-dollar Hollywood show, it was simply the result of ordinary people switching on the lights in their own homes. When we choose to do the more loving thing in our ordinary lives, we are switch-ing on a little light that will make its own unique contribution to the flow of God's love through our world.

The currency is in our own pockets: little acts of kindness, gentle words of encouragement, small gestures that make a very big difference. We can never pay back to God his immeasurable love towards us, but we can 'pay it forward' to the next person we meet who is in need of it.

Reflection

God says just one thing to us in our dealings with each other:
'Give them my love.'

MS

1 Kings 1—4: a new beginning

These chapters tell a tale of kings and kingmaking. We meet plotting princes and crafty courtiers, politicians and priests, the fading embers of an old king and the rising star of a new one. We go backstage in the royal palace, amid the manoeuvring of hangers-on. Then, we come out into the light of a new reign, rich with potential and bright with promise.

The scene is Jerusalem, a thousand years before the time of Jesus. King David lies sick. His life has almost run its course—from shepherd boy to warrior, outlaw to king, Bethlehem to Jerusalem and anointing to old age. If we follow David through the two books of Samuel, we see him achieve much in public life. He ruled his land, but could not control his sons, however, so left a split and quarrelsome household, its members vying for power. God had once given him grand promises about his family and their future. As the story moves from the books of Samuel into Kings, God's grace has to work in a deeply divided home.

Solomon, we shall see, emerges as his father's choice. From birth he was called 'Beloved of the Lord' (2 Samuel 12:25 footnote). He would establish the kingdom, build a house for God and know God as Father (7:12–14). From the start he is humble and wise, prayerful and prosperous. Before long he did indeed build 'a house for the name of the Lord' (1 Kings 5:5). Worship was a priority for Solomon.

Yet, there is a hint that this man had too many interests of his own. He was good at organising his land, but also at gathering goods for himself. Marrying a foreign princess might have forged a political alliance, but it did little for his faith. As time went by, wealth and women cast a spell over Solomon. He increased—of that there is no doubt—but sadly God decreased in his life.

A new beginning is a precious opportunity, but you need to press on, grow into new responsibility and carry it humbly. In these chapters, Solomon makes a strong start, forging on, yet his full story leaves a hollow sound in the ear, the aftertaste of a rich flavour gone sour. It leaves us longing for the one to come, who would truly be called 'Son of God'.

John Proctor

Cold comfort

Now King David was old and advanced in years; and although they covered him with clothes, he could not get warm. Therefore his servants said to him, 'Let a young maiden be sought for my lord the king, and let her wait upon the king, and be his nurse; let her lie in your bosom, that my lord the king may be warm.' So they… found Abishag the Shunammite… and she became the king's nurse and ministered to him; but the king knew her not.

This pathetic little story is an odd start to a book. The king lay sick. His courtiers made a desperate attempt to revive him by finding a kind of human hot-water bottle. They might have done better to hire an experienced nurse, for Abishag seems to have been a woman used. Part of her youth was stolen, to fend off the king's old age in a curious and unnatural relationship.

'The king knew her not' means that they had no sexual relationship, but there is much more that David does not know. The plotting of the palace and the ambitions of his son Adonijah all seem to pass him by. His time for careful and considered planning is past. People come to his bedside to claim old promises rather than draw on any fresh wisdom.

King David's old age was not handled well. His strength was failing, his sons were starting to jostle for position and the people around him dreaded the vacuum that he would leave. They dared not face the inevitable, so they tried to rescue the situation, but they did so in a manner that seems foolish and humiliating.

Growing older is a gift, but also a responsibility. A sign of ageing, they say, is when you stoop to tie a shoelace and find yourself thinking, 'Now what else can I do while I'm down here?' but there are serious concerns, too. Life goes by, energy gives way to experience, and skills that we once deployed well start to slip away from us. Let us ask for grace to receive those times as coming from God and meet them honestly and humbly. With God's help, even a period of declining strength may be an occasion for wise decisions and faithful service.

Prayer

God of all our ages, help us to respect old age and meet it without fear.

JP

Party politics

Now Adonijah son of Haggith exalted himself, saying, 'I will be king'; he prepared for himself chariots and horsemen, and fifty men to run before him. His father had never at any time displeased him by asking, 'Why have you done thus and so?' He was also a very handsome man, and he was born next after Absalom. He conferred with Joab son of Zeruiah and with the priest Abiathar... Adonijah sacrificed sheep, oxen, and fatted cattle by the stone Zoheleth, which is beside En-rogel, and he invited all his brothers, the king's sons, and all the royal officials of Judah, but he did not invite the prophet Nathan or Benaiah or the warriors or his brother Solomon.

Adonijah was the fourth son in the king's family (2 Samuel 3:4), but by now he was the eldest surviving, which put him in pole position—he hoped—to become David's heir. He had usually been able to get his own way in life, so now—with charm, wealth and shrewd advisers—he was ready to bid for the throne. Image mattered and Adonijah had style. Support mattered, too, so the sacrifice was not just a party but, rather, a way to gather allies and stake his claim to power with a solemn ceremony. If God was on Adonijah's side, who could deny him?

Most of Adonijah's younger brothers were present as he reckoned that they would fall into line with his plans, but a couple of David's top courtiers were missing. The prophet Nathan had nerve and a way with words (2 Samuel 12), while Benaiah commanded a regiment. Neither of them liked Adonijah and he was wary of them. Solomon, too, made him anxious. If anyone could derail Adonijah's bid, it would be Solomon.

So, as the scene shifts away from David's sickbed and out to the royal picnic, we realise that battle lines are being drawn. Adonijah is spoilt, selfish and showy. Solomon is silent, but the quiet man, the one who misses the party, is the man to watch. Before long, Adonijah's champagne will go flat, his bubble will burst. Pride often comes before a fall. Showing off, scheming and splitting people up in order to control them are never methods that God is likely to honour.

Prayer

Pray for the leaders of your own land and ask God to give them humility.

JP

Pillow talk

Then Nathan said to Bathsheba, Solomon's mother, 'Have you not heard that Adonijah son of Haggith has become king and our lord David does not know it? Now therefore come, let me give you advice, so that you may save your own life and the life of your son Solomon. Go in at once to King David, and say to him, "Did you not, my lord the king, swear to your servant, saying: Your son Solomon shall succeed me as king, and he shall sit on my throne? Why then is Adonijah king?" Then while you are still there speaking with the king, I will come in after you and confirm your words.'

The Bible has two parallel accounts of this stage in Israel's life. The account in Chronicles shows, much more clearly than the earlier version in Samuel and Kings, that David had been planning for Solomon to follow him as king (1 Chronicles 23:1; 29:1). This is the point on which Nathan and Bathsheba rely. The have privileged access to the royal bedroom and the king's ear. They realise that the situation has become critical and they do all they can to influence the outcome.

It is an odd alliance. Bathsheba was the woman who caught David's eye on a city rooftop (2 Samuel 11) and Nathan the prophet who challenged the king over his adultery. Bathsheba lost the child she conceived that day, but when another son was born, Nathan sensed God's special favour at work. 'This one is beloved of the Lord', he said (see 12:25).

As David grew old, Nathan and Bathsheba had a common cause. They wanted to press the case for Solomon—the child of her womb and his prophecy. This was the favoured son, they said, the one David always intended to succeed him. The king was just alert enough to respond. Sick as he was, he had enough energy to make one last big decision.

So Solomon was carried to the throne on a mother's love and a prophet's faith. He had a big debt of trust to repay. The same applies to many a duty in life—in work, at home, church, among friends. Responsibility comes because people believe in us, which is always a solemn trust, never just a matter of position, promotion or power.

Prayer

God of faithfulness, when people trust me, help me to be trustworthy.

JP

Rising son

David said, 'Summon to me the priest Zadok, the prophet Nathan, and Benaiah son of Jehoiada.' ... The king said to them, 'Take with you the servants of your lord, and have my son Solomon ride on my own mule, and bring him down to Gihon. There let the priest Zadok and the prophet Nathan anoint him king over Israel; then blow the trumpet, and say, 'Long live King Solomon!' You shall go up following him. Let him enter and sit on my throne: he shall be king in my place; for I have appointed him to be ruler over Israel and over Judah.'

David had seemed out of touch with the machinations going on around him, yet suddenly he got a grip on the situation. Solomon had to be declared king in a way that would leave the public in no doubt. Adonijah offered a sacrifice; let Solomon be anointed. Adonijah was out in the country; let Solomon be brought to the palace and placed on the throne. Adonijah had 50 men to escort his chariot; let Solomon have the royal mount, with Benaiah and the palace guard for security.

Gihon was a spring, just outside Jerusalem, nearer to the city than Enrogel, where Adonijah's group met. The trumpet would attract attention, so people would gather round. Priest and prophet would speak their prayer and promise to God. Soldiers would show strength. This had to be a proper coronation, a credible anointing.

What makes this ceremony different from Adonijah's? Certainly David's authority still counted and Solomon had his father's backing and blessing. There is a sense, too, that Solomon was destined for this. He had neither sought it nor brought it about: it was others who recognised him and raised him up. Adonijah was all style and no substance. Solomon, in contrast, was a man the people could trust.

Many of the kingly ideals in the Old Testament find their truest home in Jesus: the king riding a donkey; God's anointed, at the waters of the Jordan; royally enthroned on a cross. If Solomon appears as a figure of hope, this was not just for his own times. His story points forward to a more glorious future, to the Son of David, Jesus.

Prayer
God of the nations, give us rulers who reflect the kingly goodness of Jesus.

JP

110

Falling star

Then all the guests of Adonijah got up trembling and went their own ways. Adonijah, fearing Solomon, got up and went to grasp the horns of the altar… saying, 'Let King Solomon swear to me first that he will not kill his servant with the sword.' So Solomon responded, 'If he proves to be a worthy man, not one of his hairs shall fall to the ground; but if wickedness is found in him, he shall die.' Then King Solomon sent to have him brought down from the altar. He came to do obeisance to King Solomon; and Solomon said to him, 'Go home.'

The trumpet sounding was an alarm call for Adonijah and his guests. 'What is this?' everyone asked, and the news soon arrived: 'Our lord King David has made Solomon king' (v. 43). The party dispersed. Adonijah's supporters had no stomach for a fight. Hitching themselves to a rising star had been one thing; backing a loser was quite another. Perhaps they remembered his brother Absalom's rebellion years before (2 Samuel 15—19). He too had a chariot and 50 men to run alongside and he ended up speared through the heart, his army scattered and slain.

Adonijah was suddenly utterly alone. He ran for sanctuary, perhaps to the 'high place' at Gibeon a few miles away. It was hardly a negotiating position, but it gave him space to speak, a chance to claim a moment of mercy. Solomon's response was wary. As long as Adonijah behaved himself—and Solomon would be the judge of that—he would be safe. One false move, though, could cost him everything.

'Go home', Solomon said, but Adonijah would never be truly at home again. Wherever he went, he would need to guard his step, his speech and his skin. Solomon had been very astute. He now had a hold over his brother, and he would keep it, yet his own hands had stayed clean. Theirs was a pretty thin sort of reconciliation, rooted in distrust, suspicion and fear. Solomon's caution may have been necessary, but it is a long way short of the Christian ideal of forgiveness.

Prayer

God of all wisdom, when I run into dispute and difficulty, help me to know when to be wary and when to take the holy risk of forgiving for Jesus' sake.

JP

Right direction

When David's time to die drew near, he charged his son Solomon, saying: 'I am about to go the way of all the earth. Be strong, be courageous, and keep the charge of the Lord your God, walking in his ways and keeping his statutes, his commandments, his ordinances, and his testimonies, as it is written in the law of Moses, so that you may prosper in all that you do and wherever you turn. Then the Lord will establish his word that he spoke concerning me: "If your heirs take heed to their way, to walk before me in faithfulness with all their heart and with all their soul, there shall not fail you a successor on the throne of Israel."'

This is David's last speech. Solomon is the son he has set on the throne and now he hands over his kingship. There is nothing here about the practical skills of kingship; what matters to David is following God's ways. For his people's sake, a king must be a lawmaker, but first he must be a lawkeeper, a man under God.

'Be strong and very courageous' was also God's challenge to Joshua after Moses died (Joshua 1:7), so David's words to Solomon echo that command. To lead people, you need to be secure in yourself and act without fear, and this comes about when a person is secure in God.

Seven different words are used above to describe God's pattern for life: charge, ways, statutes, commandments, ordinances, testimonies, law. To speak in sevens recalls the opening of Genesis, as if to say, 'This is a new start, a fresh creation.' Israel will find new life and joy, her days will be good and glad and her land full of beauty and bounty, if Solomon follows God's word.

God had promised David that his kingdom would last (2 Samuel 7:12–16), but such a promise can only be upheld one stage at a time. Solomon was now to carry the baton of duty and hope. He was called to be faithful, for his father's sake and that of future generations. God calls individuals to serve him, but we always serve as part of a community, shaped by the past and the future stretching out before us.

Prayer

Pray for people younger than you, to whom you hand on a Christian example.

JP

Marked men

[David continued] 'Moreover you know also what Joab son of Zeruiah did to me, how he dealt with the two commanders of the armies of Israel, Abner son of Ner, and Amasa son of Jether, whom he murdered, retaliating in time of peace for blood that had been shed in war, and putting the blood of war on the belt around his waist, and on the sandals on his feet. Act therefore according to your wisdom, but do not let his grey head go down to Sheol in peace. Deal loyally, however, with the sons of Barzillai the Gileadite, and let them be among those who eat at your table; for with such loyalty they met me when I fled from your brother Absalom.'

After his words about faithfulness, David warns Solomon about people he will have to deal with. Events had left a mark in his memory and there are concerns that he wants to pass on. These might seem mere personal issues—gratitude and grudges, cherished in an old man's heart—but the unity and well-being of his kingdom and its people were at stake. Give the wrong people their head and the country could fragment.

Although Joab had been David's top general, he was headstrong and vindictive, a difficult man to control. On a couple of occasions he had killed a rival commander (2 Samuel 3:27; 20:9–10) when David might have found a way of bringing the two men together. More recently, he had backed Adonijah (1 Kings 1:7). Now he could be a very loose cannon around the young king Solomon. Governing the kingdom in unity and peace would never be straightforward if Joab remained at large.

Barzillai, on the other hand, was a name with happier associations. He owned land beyond the Jordan and, when David was fleeing Absalom's rebel forces, he brought food and encouragement (2 Samuel 17:27–29). At a time when the kingdom was weak and the lords on the east bank of the Jordan might have broken free from David's rule, Barzillai spoke for unity and peace. If Solomon was to govern well and claim the loyalty of the whole realm, this was a connection to value.

Reflection

What can I do to help strengthen and unite my family, my church or my community?

JP

Grace and grievance

Then David slept with his ancestors, and was buried in the city of David… So Solomon sat on the throne of his father David; and his kingdom was firmly established. Then Adonijah son of Haggith came to Bathsheba, Solomon's mother… He said, 'You know that the kingdom was mine, and that all Israel expected me to reign; however, the kingdom has turned about and become my brother's, for it was his from the Lord… Please ask King Solomon—he will not refuse you—to give me Abishag the Shunammite as my wife.' Bathsheba said, 'Very well; I will speak to the king on your behalf.'

The Bible often shows us a handover of grace from one generation to another. It is a constant process, as steady as the changing of the seasons, yet sometimes we see it in sharp focus in a particular transition. Moses to Joshua is one, Elijah to Elisha another and, here, David to Solomon. Solomon's kingdom was established. This had been God's promise, repeated three times to David (2 Samuel 7:12–16). Anyone tracing the whole story is surely meant to hear the echo. God is delivering on his pledge. Solomon will reign securely because God has put him there.

Adonijah must have been either a mischief-maker or very stupid. Abishag had been the old king's companion, keeping him warm in bed, an intimate in almost every way. To marry her would be a public sign that Adonijah was David's rightful heir. It would undermine Solomon's position, suggesting that his older brother was the real king-to-be. Did he not realise how his request would appear? Why did he work through Bathsheba—to manipulate Solomon, bypassing his suspicions?

The ploy was ill-advised: it cost Adonijah his life (2:22–25). Solomon was determined to defend his new reign, firmly and fiercely. Bathsheba, too, was unwise to get involved. Proverbs 26:17 says that meddling in someone else's quarrel is like seizing a passing dog by the ears. You irritate people and rarely do any good. A wise church leader once said, 'I never mediate in a dispute, unless asked to do so by both sides.'

Prayer

May God give me wisdom to understand myself, to deal properly with other people and to know when to be silent.

JP

1 KINGS 3:1–3 (NRSV)

Foundations for the future

Solomon made a marriage alliance with Pharaoh king of Egypt; he took Pharaoh's daughter and brought her into the city of David, until he had finished building his own house and the house of the Lord and the wall around Jerusalem. The people were sacrificing at the high places, however, because no house had yet been built for the name of the Lord. Solomon loved the Lord, walking in the statutes of his father David; only, he sacrificed and offered incense at the high places.

We have moved on half a chapter since yesterday's passage. The new king is ceasing to be new and settling into the role. Now we shall see what sort of king he makes. The main impression will be positive and praiseworthy—yet that is not the whole story.

A royal marriage is often a shrewd political move. When neighbouring royal families are linked in marriage, both kings work hard to sustain good relations. The frontier will be secure, trade can flourish and each nation has a natural ally. When Solomon married the princess of Egypt, he may have been motivated as much by political gain as by romance.

Building was another project to embrace. The king wanted a proper palace for himself and his bride, as well as a centre for the nation's worship and a decent set of city defences. Of these three, the prime issue would surely have been that of providing a place of worship. God had promised that David's successor would build a temple (2 Samuel 7:13). This would become a solid sign of Israel's commitment to the Lord. As a family of faith, loving God was the core of the people's life together. Solomon would help them to make this love visible.

Is there a hint, as the king sets to work, that all is not well? Solomon's many foreign wives eventually diluted his faith (11:1–8). The palace turned out to be the more elaborate of the two buildings (chs. 6—7), and the 'high places' undermined Israel's religious commitment for generations. Solomon 'loved the Lord', but perhaps not deeply enough.

Prayer

God of every new beginning and opportunity, help me to grasp each moment and each duty in ways that express my loyalty and love to you.

JP

Wishing well

At Gibeon the Lord appeared to Solomon in a dream by night; and God said, 'Ask what I should give you.' And Solomon said, 'You have shown great and steadfast love to your servant my father David, because he walked before you in faithfulness... And now, O Lord my God, you have made your servant king in place of my father David, although I am only a little child; I do not know how to go out or come in... Give your servant therefore an understanding mind to govern your people, able to discern between good and evil; for who can govern this your great people?'

As I have read the early chapters of 1 Kings and dipped into some commentaries, two portraits of Solomon have emerged. They do not really match. One has a bright, honest face—a prince of promise, whose life God touched with goodness and grace. He was God's choice for the throne and he ruled with poise, blessing and success. This is the Solomon we see in today's reading. He approaches the king's task with faith and humility and asks God for wisdom.

The other portrait has more warts. It is Solomon in the untidy world of politics, coping with power, money, success and popularity. Despite his faith he stumbles, compromises and eventually falls some way short of the highest ideals and standards. So, which face of Solomon do you see—faith or flaws?

Perhaps we ought to take both portraits seriously. Like most people, Solomon did not always live up to God's ideals. His life was pushed out of shape by circumstance, conflict and temptation. If he seems a divided personality, he is very like some of us. Neither our highest hopes nor our biggest mistakes tell the whole truth about us. Faith is about living with our tangled selves and letting God deal with us as we are.

Like Solomon, we need to know the difference between good and evil (v. 9). The wisdom he asked for is a gift from God and, if it shapes our own lives, we shall offer something of God to other people, too.

Reflection

'I am only a little child', Soloman says. Do you feel like this when you meet with God? How does God respond to trusting and humble people?

JP

Awake to God

God said to him, 'Because you have asked this, and have not asked for yourself long life or riches, or for the life of your enemies, but have asked for yourself understanding to discern what is right, I now do according to your word. Indeed I give you a wise and discerning mind… I give you also what you have not asked, both riches and honour all your life; no other king shall compare with you. If you will walk in my ways, keeping my statutes and my commandments, as your father David walked, then I will lengthen your life.' Then Solomon awoke; it had been a dream.

Solomon asked to know the difference between good and evil (v. 9) and God gave him that gift. Adam and Eve had wanted this, too (Genesis 3:1–7), but they soon found they had bitten off more than they could chew. So why was Solomon allowed to receive wisdom? The difference is surely that real wisdom can never be grasped; it can only be given. It is never ours to possess, but is always a gift, a treasure on loan from heaven. Solomon knew he needed this ability, that without it his kingship would founder.

There is a long and loud echo of this passage in the book of Proverbs, where the first nine chapters say, in a multitude of different ways, 'Get wisdom'. It is like a rerun of Solomon's prayer. Wisdom is the key to living well. 'Long life is in her right hand; in her left hand are riches and honour' (3:16). Wisdom is reflected in God's good creation. We meet it in the advice and care of faithful people. You hear it in your own conscience. You follow it in the things you say, the company you keep, the deeds you do and the promises you keep.

'Solomon awoke; it had been a dream', yet it had been more real, with more light in it, than many a waking thought or encounter. Perhaps it was in sleep, in the sanctuary—on retreat, we might say—that Solomon had been truly open to God. God was there, drawing out his deepest thoughts and hopes and prayers.

Reflection

'The darkness is not dark to you; the night is as bright as the day'
(Psalm 139:12).

JP

Whose baby?

Two women... came to the king and stood before him. One woman said, 'Please, my lord, this woman and I live in the same house... this woman's son died in the night, because she lay on him. She got up in the middle of the night and took my son... and laid her dead son at my breast.'... So they argued before the king... So the king said, 'Bring me a sword... Divide the living boy in two; then give half to the one, and half to the other.' But the woman whose son was alive said to the king—because compassion for her son burned within her—'Please, my lord, give her the living boy...' Then the king responded: 'Give the first woman the living boy; do not kill him. She is his mother.'

How could anyone tell which of the two mothers was telling the truth? Both claimed the living child was theirs and there were no witnesses to support either woman's word. The king was chief justice in Israel, so he had to find a way forward.

Now God's wisdom was being put into practice. Solomon had been granted wisdom in a dream, yet the gift went with him into his life in the morning and on through the years. It was given in a place of worship, but would be used in the everyday, unexpected and perplexing. He cuts through the tangle of uncertainty and deceit and brings a mother's love into plain view. The baby's mother would rather he were given to someone else than put to death. The bereaved woman could not see past her own loss and so tried to drag her neighbour down, too, saying, 'It shall be neither mine nor yours; divide it' (v. 26).

Is it just a story? Just history? Not really. Bereavement does strange things to people. Losing a child can be a dreadful blow to bear. If some behave oddly—even very wrongly—at such a time, who are most of us to judge? Not Solomon, it seems. He restores, but (so far as we can see) does not punish. What would you have done?

Prayer

Pray for parents who have lost a child, for people who must make decisions about child custody and care and children who are drawn into adult disputes.

JP

People at peace

Judah and Israel were as numerous as the sand by the sea; they ate and drank and were happy. Solomon was sovereign over all the kingdoms from the Euphrates to the land of the Philistines, even to the border of Egypt; they brought tribute and served Solomon all the days of his life… During Solomon's lifetime Judah and Israel lived in safety, from Dan even to Beer-sheba, all of them under their vines and fig trees. Solomon also had forty thousand stalls of horses for his chariots, and twelve thousand horsemen.

The whole of this chapter tells of the start of Solomon's reign in an upbeat and hopeful tone. God gave him wisdom and he started to use it. Yesterday we saw him dealing with a very personal sadness. Today, the camera of scripture takes a more wide-angled view, looking across the kingdom to find a whole people living in prosperity and peace.

Its borders were broad and secure, stretching out to north, east and south. After David's years of expansion, a wide area of land lay under the king's control. Solomon, though, proved to be a builder more than a military man. Gathering, government, order and organisation were his strengths. Indeed, if we read the earlier part of this chapter, we see a web of royal officials bringing in food for the king's household. Government costs, but if it is done properly, it should not cost the people's well-being or trust. Solomon's rule is portrayed as a time when the people and palace had plenty, and the nation grew rich along with the king.

Responsible rule gives people safety, a sense that they can trust their leaders and the freedom to concentrate on work and well-being. The land can be farmed and the community fed. Families will flourish and friends feast. The only hint of a shadow side to the regime is Solomon's hefty contingent of cavalry. Israel's kings had been warned against accumulating horses (Deuteronomy 17:16). This would make them too dependent on foreign lands. Stables don't give you stability; faith and obedience do that.

Prayer

*Pray for those who govern your land, that they will work
for the well-being of all the people.*

JP

Word and image

God gave Solomon very great wisdom, discernment, and breadth of understanding as vast as the sand on the seashore, so that Solomon's wisdom surpassed the wisdom of all the people of the east, and all the wisdom of Egypt. He was wiser than anyone else... his fame spread throughout all the surrounding nations. He composed three thousand proverbs, and his songs numbered a thousand and five. He would speak of trees, from the cedar that is in the Lebanon to the hyssop that grows in the wall; he would speak of animals, and birds, and reptiles, and fish.

Wisdom is a many-sided jewel. By wisdom, 'kings reign, and rulers decree what is just' (Proverbs 8:15). As we have already seen, wisdom guided Solomon in judgment and equipped him to rule. Today's verses show another side of wisdom. She is a good teacher, helping people to understand and enjoy the world and live sensibly and confidently within it.

Solomon the teacher was a man of image and invention, borrowing his pictures from nature in all its beauty and bounty. In different ways, three Old Testament books pass on his legacy: pithy Proverbs, full of practical one-liners; the perplexity of Ecclesiastes and the heady love poetry of the Song of Songs. For example, 'Go to the ant' to learn about work (Proverbs 6:6), 'All is vanity and a chasing after wind' (Ecclesiastes 1:14) and 'Your kisses [are] like the best wine' (Song of Soloman 7:9).

God's good creation is a classroom if we use it well. The turning seasons are a moving picture of earth's delights and demands. There are many marks of the maker's hand, acting as signposts to heaven amid the days and years. Solomon learned in this classroom and passed on his insight to many. So did one 'greater than Solomon' (Matthew 12:42). Jesus also looked at nature and spoke of God. He planted faith in the ground of experience. His sayings were like burrs, sticking to our minds and coming home with us. 'Consider the lilies,' he said, and 'strive first for the kingdom of God' (Matthew 6:28, 33).

Prayer

God of creation, thank you for your lovely world. God of love, thank you for Jesus. God of Jesus, thank you for coming among us and staying with us.

JP

John 6—8

As we read the four Gospels in the New Testament, we see both similarities and differences between them. We also notice that Matthew, Mark and Luke are more similar to one another than they are to John. Scholars think that these similarities and differences arise out of different source material and authorship. Leaving such technicalities to one side, most of them agree that the Gospel of John was probably written later than the other three. By this time, the Church was much more Gentile in its membership and John joins the dots between Jesus' ministry and the Old Testament in a way that the other three Gospels do not.

John's Gospel can open up whole new depths of meaning for us and, as John himself says, this was his intention. His Gospel was written, 'That you may believe that Jesus is the Christ, the Son of God, and that by believing you may have life in his name' (20:31). He links the promise to be found in Jesus with the promises of God in the Old Testament and, as we make these connections, John gives us a rich experience of Jesus' words and deeds.

John does not, however, paint a false, rosy picture. He makes it plain that Jesus' teaching was often misunderstood and that even those closest to him missed the point. For John, Jesus' miracles were signs—events that had a deeper meaning. As he describes them he points out that, all too often, people were captivated by the extraordinary things that Jesus did but failed to see the truth behind them. When Jesus declared the truth to which his miracles pointed, the opinions of the people around him were divided.

John's Gospel, the fourth Gospel, is not merely an historical account of what Jesus did and said but also a witness to Jesus. John wanted us to know what Jesus meant and why he did what he did. His concern was not only to show us that Jesus' mission culminated in the 'hour of his glorification' (12:27–28) but also to challenge us to make a judgment about Jesus. When we read John's Gospel, it's as if we are standing in the crowd, listening to Jesus, watching what he does, while our neighbour, standing beside us (John), nudges us, nods towards Jesus and says, 'I know you hear him and see him, but do you see? Do you really see?'

David Robertson

Sunday 15 August

JOHN 6:5–6, 10–14 (NIV, ABRIDGED)

A Passover meal

When Jesus looked up and saw a great crowd coming towards him, he said to Philip, 'Where shall we buy bread for these people to eat?' He asked this only to test him, for he already had in mind what he was going to do... Jesus said, 'Make the people sit down'... and they sat down, about five thousand of them. Jesus then took the loaves, gave thanks, and distributed to those who were seated as much as they wanted. He did the same with the fish. When they had all had enough to eat... [the disciples] filled twelve baskets with the pieces of the five barley loaves left over by those who had eaten. After the people saw the miraculous sign that Jesus did, they began to say, 'Surely this is the Prophet who is to come into the world.'

Crowds of people were following Jesus and their motivation was probably mixed. Some—whom we could call the 'back-row people'—were hoping to see exciting healings (v. 2), while others (the front-row people) would have twigged that something important and godly was going on.

On this occasion, everyone not only saw something extraordinary but they also ate it! What they saw and ate, though, wasn't just miraculous food or a test of Philip's understanding—it was a test for everyone. They saw what Jesus did with the bread and fish, but did they understand? Did they really see? Did they make the connection between this miraculous meal and the Passover feast (Exodus 12:21–28) when they would celebrate the annual Passover meal and look forward, with hope, to the time when God would send the Messiah? John tells us that they saw enough to wonder about Jesus.

Whatever their original motivations, these people witnessed something that made them think. Jesus' miracle cut across their expectations and became a sign that spoke to both the front and back rows. Maybe in our churches it doesn't matter if the back rows are more heavily populated than the front ones. Perhaps it is no concern of ours if some of those who come do so with mixed motives. When Jesus is present, he cuts across our expectations with signs that challenge us all.

Reflection
Am I a back- or front-row person? Does it matter?

DR

A new crossing

When evening came, his disciples went down to the lake, where they got into a boat and set off across the lake for Capernaum. By now it was dark, and Jesus had not yet joined them. A strong wind was blowing and the waters grew rough. When they had rowed three or three and a half miles, they saw Jesus approaching the boat, walking on the water; and they were terrified. But he said to them, 'It is I; don't be afraid.' Then they were willing to take him into the boat, and immediately the boat reached the shore where they were heading.

In John's Gospel, this miracle, which follows the feeding of the five thousand, is connected with the exodus. After Passover, God miraculously parted the Red Sea so that the people might cross from slavery to freedom (Exodus 14). In subsequent generations, every aspect of this journey came to represent the spiritual journey from the slavery of sin to the freedom of forgiveness. Here, Jesus walks not through parted waters (where the people can follow), but across the lake (where he alone can go). In John's Gospel, miracles are signs to be seen and understood (20:30–31). Jesus feeds the people and then walks over the lake: here is a new Passover meal and a new crossing from sin to forgiveness.

The disciples, of course, have no idea what's happening. They see someone walking where he should sink and their brains reject what their eyes are seeing. It's only when they understand that this impossible person is Jesus that they welcome him into the boat. As we clergy say, there's a sermon there, isn't there? Do we tend, in our evangelistic endeavours, to paint Jesus in the most attractive light possible? If we do, then we may be handing people a portrait of Jesus instead of encouraging them to meet the risen Christ. When he comes, it's on his own terms and he can be terrifying from a distance—until we recognise him.

Back in the boat, the disciples must have been looking sideways at Jesus and each other. The sign, though, was there to be understood: here's the one who can make the impossible journey from sin to forgiveness.

Prayer
Lord, when your actions trouble me, let me know that it is you.

DR

JOHN 6:25–29 (NIV)

People seek Jesus

When [the crowd] found him on the other side of the lake, they asked him, 'Rabbi, when did you get here?' Jesus answered, 'I tell you the truth, you are looking for me, not because you saw miraculous signs but because you ate the loaves and had your fill. Do not work for food that spoils, but for food that endures to eternal life, which the Son of Man will give you. On him God the Father has placed his seal of approval.' Then they asked him, 'What must we do to do the works God requires?' Jesus answered, 'The work of God is this: to believe in the one he has sent.'

On Sunday, we noted that, on many occasions, Jesus didn't seem to mind whether people were front- or back-row people. In today's reading, though, he did. When the people ate the bread and fish, it led them to wonder if Jesus was the Messiah. They had seen the sign and looked towards where it was pointing. Now, after a good night's sleep, they seem to have forgotten about the spiritual import of their experience and are solely concerned with breakfast! It seems that everyone has become a member of the back-row brigade overnight and you can imagine Jesus heaving a heavy sigh!

Human nature can be very frustrating. Years ago, the vicar of a neighbouring church experienced spiritual renewal and discovered a remarkable healing ministry. During this time, my colleague was asked to conduct a funeral and met the bereaved family, including the grandmother, who had a serious illness. He bravely asked if a small group of people from his church could pray with her. The family said, 'Yes please' and they did so. The old lady was healed completely and the Christians were ecstatic, but the family and the grandmother took the whole incident in their stride. They were happy that she was better, but didn't see any reason to adjust their view of God, visit the church or change their lives. In John's terms, they saw the sign, but didn't look any further. Hence, Jesus' answer when the people ask, 'What must we do?': 'Believe in me.' The miracles are signs. Unless we see who it is that they are pointing at, we've missed the point.

Prayer
Lord, help me see.

DR

The best thing since sliced manna

So they asked him, 'What miraculous sign then will you give that we may see it and believe you? What will you do? Our ancestors ate the manna in the desert; as it is written: "He gave them bread from heaven to eat."' Jesus said to them, 'I tell you the truth, it is not Moses who has given you the bread from heaven, but it is my Father who gives you the true bread from heaven. For the bread of God is he who comes down from heaven and gives life to the world.' 'Sir,' they said, 'from now on give us this bread.' Then Jesus declared, 'I am the bread of life. Whoever comes to me will never go hungry, and whoever believes in me will never be thirsty.'

In today's reading, Jesus joins the dots so that the big picture emerges. The people have already seen, and eaten, a miraculous sign but they, like the family mentioned yesterday, don't see this as a reason to believe in Jesus. Neither do they connect the bread and fish they enjoyed with the Passover and freedom. They want something clear, like the miracle of manna. They're struggling with Jesus because everything that he says and does leaves them baffled. They find themselves listening to him, watching him and being left with a sense of 'What's this?' Instead, they want manna, like their ancestors.

The joke is on them. Exodus 16 recounts the first occasion when God fed his people with manna. On that first morning, they looked out of their tents, had no idea what the flaky stuff on the ground was, so they called to each other, 'What's this?' (in their language, 'Manna?') Moses understood what the flaky stuff was and told them that it was the bread promised by God and that they should eat it. They did, and they gave the flaky bread a nickname: 'What's this?' or 'manna'.

When God provides, human beings are often baffled. His provision might be bread in the desert or Jesus, who feeds five thousand men with just five loaves and two fish, but the human reaction to these actions is to ask, 'What's this?' God's answer is, 'It's "What's this!" Eat it. It's the manna of life.'

Prayer

Lord Jesus, you are the answer to my hunger and thirst.

DR

Hard teaching

Then the Jews began to argue sharply among themselves, 'How can this man give us his flesh to eat?' Jesus said to them, 'I tell you the truth, unless you eat the flesh of the Son of Man and drink his blood, you have no life in you... This is the bread that came down from heaven. Your ancestors ate manna and died, but whoever feeds on this bread will live for ever.'... On hearing it, many of his disciples said, 'This is a hard teaching. Who can accept it?'... From this time many of his disciples turned back and no longer followed him.

Have you come across the phrase, 'This is where the rubber hits the road'? It originates in the car industry: an engine is useless until its power can be turned into motion through the tyres. It's widely used to talk about putting theory into practice, and that's what's happening in today's passage. The people have already asked, 'What must we do?' and Jesus has told them, 'Believe in me.' The next question is, 'What, then, must we believe?' and the answer is, 'That I am the bread of life, the new manna, which gives life not for one day but for eternity.' That is when the rubber hits the road.

It's possible to read the other Gospels and get the impression that Jesus went from early success to general acclamation—until his arrest and crucifixion, when his support suddenly evaporated. John tells the story differently. His Gospel is overshadowed by the final phase of Jesus' ministry, and God's provision (Jesus) is rejected throughout. The people are hungry for miracles, but not for the bread of life. They want to experience God, but not on his terms. They are, in effect, excited by the power of God, but when the rubber hits the road in the person of Jesus, they crash, give up and turn back.

For the last few days, we've been thinking about those who see, but look no further. Today, we are introduced to those who see clearly and then say, 'No.' This does not change God's provision, however. Jesus is the bread of life for everyone; there is no other bread. He is where the rubber hits the road.

Prayer

Lord, when your teaching is hard, help me to accept it.

DR

What of you?

'You do not want to leave too, do you?' Jesus asked the Twelve. Simon Peter answered him, 'Lord, to whom shall we go? You have the words of eternal life. We believe and know that you are the Holy One of God.' Then Jesus replied, 'Have I not chosen you, the Twelve? Yet one of you is a devil!' (He meant Judas, the son of Simon Iscariot, who, though one of the Twelve, was later to betray him.) After this, Jesus went around in Galilee, purposely staying away from Judea because the Jews there were waiting to take his life.

As we have seen, John connects these passages with the Passover, so this conversation relates to a wilderness experience, an associated theme. When the Israelites left Egypt, they left their lives as slaves, but embarked on a new life that was not always to their taste. Despite God's provision, they often looked back to their days in Egypt with longing! They wanted the land ahead, but didn't much fancy the wilderness through which they had to journey to reach it. That is the pattern of Jesus' ministry at this point. Many who have journeyed with him have gone back to their previous lives, so Jesus asks his disciples, 'What about you?'

Some people seem to sail through life (and faith) with little more than the occasional ripple to disturb their serenity. For the rest of us, though, following Jesus can be tough. For the disciples, answering this question was a crossroads moment. Would they also leave?

Peter seems to be the spokesman and he doesn't try to jolly the boss along with a hearty, 'Don't be discouraged. All those who've left are back-row people anyway! We're the front row and we're still here!' His answer is disarmingly honest. He doesn't deny that Jesus' teaching is hard, but accepts it and says, 'You are the one God has sent; where else can we go?'

As Christians, there are times in our lives when we have a wilderness experience and say, 'This is too hard.' If God has led us there, though, that's all that matters. If we are with Jesus, where else can we go but forward with him?

Reflection

A desert is a wilderness without water. A wilderness experience only becomes a desert when Jesus, the water of life, is not there.

DR

Helpful advice?

When the Jewish Feast of Tabernacles was near, Jesus' brothers said to him, 'You ought to leave here and go to Judea, so that your disciples may see the miracles you do. No one who wants to become a public figure acts in secret. Since you are doing these things, show yourself to the world.' For even his own brothers did not believe in him. Therefore Jesus told them, 'The right time for me has not yet come; for you any time is right. The world cannot hate you, but it hates me because I testify that what it does is evil. You go to the Feast. I am not yet going up to this Feast, because for me the right time has not yet come.' Having said this, he stayed in Galilee.

It's clear from this reading that Jesus' brothers could have worked in a PR agency. What they advise (how best to promote celebrity) is standard practice today and if PR agents didn't do just this, only people with talent would come to public notice. John tells us, however, that Jesus' brothers gave this advice cynically. They didn't believe in Jesus, so their words were a challenge: 'Go to Jerusalem and prove youself!'

The context of this abrasive exchange is the Feast of Tabernacles, some six months after Passover. The theme of the festival was still linked to the Exodus, tabernacles (tents or booths) being erected on rooftops or in gardens and courtyards with people living in them for a week as a remembrance of their ancestors' journey through the wilderness. These tabernacles were a sign of faith—trusting God in the impermanence of life—and many people travelled to Jerusalem to observe the feast and give thanks for the grape harvest.

Jesus tells his brothers to go without him. They have no faith in him, so it's better that they go and live in their tabernacle and express their faith through a tradition which looks back to God's provision in the past. Jesus is the one in whom a living faith may be found in the present and for the future, but because they are only looking back, they cannot see Jesus for who he is.

Prayer

Lord we have rich traditions, but may their richness never cloud our vision of you.

DR

Sunday 22 August

John 7:10, 14–17, 24 (NIV)

Make a right judgment

However, after his brothers had left for the Feast, he went also, not publicly, but in secret... Not until halfway through the Feast did Jesus go up to the temple courts and begin to teach. The Jews were amazed and asked, 'How did this man get such learning without having studied?' Jesus answered, 'My teaching is not my own. It comes from him who sent me. Anyone who chooses to do the will of God will find out whether my teaching comes from God or whether I speak on my own... Stop judging by mere appearances, and make a right judgment.'

Having sent his brothers to the festival, Jesus then goes, too. For the first few days, he, like everyone else, would have been reflecting on the exodus while living in a tent made of palm leaves. Then he is prompted to go to the temple. Teachers would be dotted around the temple courts and Jesus would find a spot, sit down and begin. If he was any good, a crowd would gather to listen, argue and question him.

Jesus proved more than good; he was amazing. John does not record his teaching, but his subject would probably have been the lessons learned from the 40 years of living in tents between Egypt and Canaan.

When Jesus is questioned about the source of his teaching, he answers simply: his teaching is from God. People must make a spiritual judgment. If they think Jesus is telling the truth, they should pay attention and live accordingly. Thus, Jesus challenges his own generation, and ours.

In March 2009, BBC crime reporter Ben Ando reported that our law courts have an increasing problem with hung juries—partly because TV dramas suggest that forensic evidence is clear-cut (it often isn't), but mostly because people feel increasingly uncomfortable about judging others. Our culture prefers to think of others as 'different', not innocent or guilty, and we like to come to the same conclusion when we judge ourselves. This is a cultural shift with a spiritual impact. If we cannot, or will not, make right judgments about our own shortcomings (sin), then we are unlikely to make right judgments about the words of Christ.

Prayer

Lord, I open my life to your judgment and mercy.

DR

Who knows?

At that point some of the people of Jerusalem began to ask, 'Isn't this the man they are trying to kill? Here he is, speaking publicly, and they are not saying a word to him. Have the authorities really concluded that he is the Christ? But we know where this man is from; when the Christ comes, no one will know where he is from.' Then Jesus, still teaching in the temple courts, cried out, 'Yes, you know me, and you know where I am from. I am not here on my own, but he who sent me is true. You do not know him, but I know him because I am from him and he sent me.' At this they tried to seize him, but no one laid a hand on him, because his time had not yet come. Still, many in the crowd put their faith in him. They said, 'When the Christ comes, will he do more miraculous signs than this man?'

The people find themselves, yet again, baffled by Jesus. His teaching is amazing and his miracles are extraordinary so all the evidence points to him being the Messiah. On the other hand, there was a common belief that the Messiah would be unknown until Elijah anointed him. They knew that Jesus was from Nazareth, so, in their minds, because Jesus' origins were known, he couldn't be the Messiah (Matthew 13:54–56), yet they heard his teaching, saw his miracles and wondered all the same. On this occasion, they speculated that the authorities knew the answer to the riddle of Jesus but hadn't told anyone.

Jesus was aware of the speculation and said, in effect, 'Yes, you know where I grew up, but you don't know where I am from. You don't recognise me because you don't know the one who sent me.' To us, this may sound like a riddle, but to the people of Jesus' time his words were crystal clear. He was claiming that God had sent him (he was accepting the title of Messiah) and as their confusion turned to anger, it threatened to become physical. They preferred their commonly held beliefs about God to the reality of God's presence among them, but, on this occasion, they could not touch Jesus as it was not 'his time'.

Reflection

Jesus always was, and still is, the capstone or a stumbling block (Luke 20:17–18).

DR

Immanuel

The Pharisees heard the crowd whispering such things about him. Then the chief priests and the Pharisees sent temple guards to arrest him. Jesus said, 'I am with you for only a short time, and then I go to the one who sent me. You will look for me, but you will not find me; and where I am, you cannot come.' The Jews said to one another, 'Where does this man intend to go that we cannot find him? Will he go where our people live scattered among the Greeks, and teach the Greeks? What did he mean when he said, "You will look for me, but you will not find me," and "Where I am, you cannot come"?'

I wonder, does the incarnation—a hot topic at Christmas—tend to drift into the background of our thinking during the rest of the year? If so, then today's reading is a timely reminder of what incarnation means.

Jesus speaks in spiritual terms. He prophesies his death and declares that, unlike the death we shall all experience, his death will be unique. It will be a journey that he alone can make; no one else can go where he is to go. Let's remember that in John's Gospel, this is still the Feast of Tabernacles and the journey of Exodus was a metaphor for the journey from sin to forgiveness and that is the journey Jesus is talking about. The people, though, interpret Jesus' words in human terms. If Jesus is going on a journey, where is he going? Athens?

This is the significance of the incarnation. When you listen to Jesus, you can listen to a man or listen to God. You can look at the sign or look at where it's pointing. Even at Jesus' crucifixion, people were making different judgments about him (Luke 23:39–43). One criminal looked sideways at Jesus, saw a man and died cursing him. The other criminal also looked at Jesus, but he saw God incarnate and died with Jesus' promise that after death he would have a new life in paradise with him. On the cross, Jesus made the journey into death, that human beings might journey from sin to forgiveness—and no one is excluded, not even a criminal who said that he deserved to be executed.

Prayer
Lord, thank you that in your death I have eternal life.

DR

Living water

On the last and greatest day of the Feast, Jesus stood and said in a loud voice, 'Let anyone who is thirsty come to me and drink. Whoever believes in me, as the Scripture has said, will have streams of living water flowing from within.' By this he meant the Spirit, whom those who believed in him were later to receive. Up to that time the Spirit had not been given, since Jesus had not yet been glorified. On hearing his words, some of the people said, 'Surely this man is the Prophet.' Others said, 'He is the Christ.'... Some wanted to seize him, but no one laid a hand on him.

The Feast of Tabernacles had its own rituals, centred on the temple. Every day, priests processed to the pool of Siloam and collected water for various ritual washings. It was also poured down the temple steps so that it flowed out of the temple as a symbol of the true faith flowing into the world. Whichever day of the week the last day of the Feast fell on, it was treated as a sabbath and the rituals reached their climax. It may well have been that while the priests were pouring water down the temple steps, Jesus shouted, 'Drink from me.'

John tells us that Jesus was talking about the Holy Spirit. When the disciples received the Holy Spirit at Pentecost (Acts 2:1–4), it was like feeling a violent wind and seeing tongues of fire. As the story of Acts unfolds, the Spirit can be thought of as moving like floodwater, bearing Jesus' message from Jerusalem into the surrounding territories—making the symbolism of water running down the temple steps a reality.

Pentecost is more than an invitation to satisfy our spiritual thirst. This one-day festival (between Passover and Tabernacles) was associated with the giving of the Law. When the Holy Spirit came upon believers at Pentecost it was a sign that the Law, written on stone tablets (Exodus 24:12) and kept in the temple (1 Kings 6:19), would now be written in the lives of those who received the Spirit. They would become a new, living temple (Ephesians 2:20–22) and God's living water would now flow as life-giving streams through the lives of believers.

Prayer

Lord Jesus, I drink in your living water. Flow through me this day.

DR

Unbelief

Finally the temple guards went back to the chief priests and Pharisees, who asked them, 'Why didn't you bring him in?' 'No one ever spoke the way this man does,' the guards declared. 'You mean he has deceived you also?' the Pharisees retorted. 'Has any of the rulers or of the Pharisees believed in him? No! But this mob that knows nothing of the law—there is a curse on them.' Nicodemus, who had gone to Jesus earlier and who was one of their own number, asked, 'Does our law condemn people without first hearing them to find out what they are doing?'

John presents us with the truth: Jesus divides everyone. Even his own followers came to different conclusions about him, as did the crowds and temple guards. The Pharisees, too, were divided. The honest answer to their question, 'Has any Pharisee believed in him?' is, 'Yes; Nicodemus!' Nicodemus does his best to stick up for Jesus while protecting his own position. It's a common experience: a powerful person makes a sweeping statement and we think, 'I don't actually agree with you', but it's very difficult to say so aloud. There are many circumstances when it's hard to declare what we believe, even when the Holy Spirit flows in us! For Nicodemus, living with a pre-Pentecost belief in Jesus, it was impossible.

The chief priests and Pharisees had made up their minds. Jesus was not the Messiah; therefore he was not from God, so his teaching was false and his miracles were deceptions. It was simple logic and it depended on that one fundamental decision: Jesus was not the Messiah. In our culture, we live with the outcome of a similar fundamental decision. At the centre of much evolutionary thought is the premise that God does not exist. Evolutionary theory (of itself, neither pro-God nor anti-God) is interpreted as upholding this decision; it then follows, logically, that the words of Jesus are lies and his miracles deceptions.

Interestingly, once the Holy Spirit began to flow through the lives of believers, many priests believed, too (Acts 6:7). I wonder if any of them were part of the discussions in today's passage.

Prayer
Lord, give me grace to speak even when it's hard.

DR

Adulterous people

The teachers of the law and the Pharisees brought in a woman caught in adultery... and said to Jesus, 'Teacher, this woman was caught in the act of adultery. In the Law Moses commanded us to stone such women. Now what do you say?'... Jesus bent down and started to write on the ground with his finger. When they kept on questioning him, he straightened up and said to them, 'Let any one of you who is without sin be the first to throw a stone at her.' Again he stooped down and wrote on the ground... Jesus straightened up and asked her, 'Woman, where are they? Has no one condemned you?' 'No one, sir,' she said. 'Then neither do I condemn you,' Jesus declared. 'Go now and leave your life of sin.'

This passage stimulates some common questions. 'What about the man? Why wasn't he dragged before Jesus, too?' The common answers are, 'He ran away!' or 'It was a sexist culture, so they treated men differently.' The likely answer, though, is that while the woman committed adultery, the man did not.

To our 21st-century minds this answer is bizarre because we think of adultery as something that we commit *with* a sexual partner. In Jesus' time, though, they thought of adultery as an act committed *against* the spouse of the sexual partner. If the woman in today's reading was unmarried, but the man she slept with had a wife, then the woman committed adultery not *with* the man but *against* his wife. He, however, did not commit adultery if the woman had no spouse. Instead, he committed the lesser sin of fornication.

This is also the biblical thinking behind the unfaithfulness of God's people when they worshipped other gods (for example, Deuteronomy 32:15–20). What they were doing *with* their sin was one thing, but what they were doing *against* God was the heart of their unfaithfulness. When human beings sin, it's a personal act against God and yet, 'God so loved the world that he gave his one and only Son, that whoever believes in him shall not perish but have eternal life. For God did not send his Son into the world to condemn the world...' (John 3:16–17).

Prayer

Thank you, Lord, that you do not condemn me.

DR

Saturday 28 August

JOHN 8:12–15, 20 (NIV)

Light of the world

When Jesus spoke again to the people, he said, 'I am the light of the world. Whoever follows me will never walk in darkness, but will have the light of life.' The Pharisees challenged him, 'Here you are, appearing as your own witness; your testimony is not valid.' Jesus answered, 'Even if I testify on my own behalf, my testimony is valid, for I know where I came from and where I am going. But you have no idea where I come from or where I am going. You judge by human standards; I pass judgment on no one...' He spoke these words while teaching in the temple area near the place where the offerings were put. Yet no one seized him, because his time had not yet come.

During the Feast of Tabernacles, as well as having water poured down the temple steps, four large lamps were erected in the temple courtyard, and the people held flaming torches. This light shone over Jerusalem, symbolising the light of the Jewish faith shining for all to see.

As there is a question mark over the chronology of John 8:1–11 (one manuscript puts it after John 7:36, others after 21:24), we should think of the content of today's passage taking place on the final day of the Feast of Tabernacles rather than on the day after (as suggested by 8:2). While the light was shining from the temple, Jesus proclaimed himself to be not only a light for Jerusalem but also the light of the world.

The Pharisees challenged him because they were locked into the idea that Jesus was not the Messiah—so he could not be any kind of light. They fell back on logic to refute him: under their law, personal testimony without corroboration was invalid. Jesus replied that they were missing the point (and the truth), that he was indeed the Messiah. He also said that, in this regard, their law was of human origin—a criticism the Pharisees regarded as blasphemy. When Jesus' time came, he was crucified for these 'blasphemies', but afterwards came the resurrection and Pentecost. Then, there were more witnesses to validate Jesus' words.

Reflection
'He has sent me to proclaim freedom for the prisoners and recovery of sight for the blind' (Luke 4:18).

DR

Sunday 29 August

JOHN 8:23–25, 27–30 (NIV)

Leap of faith

[Jesus] continued, 'You are from below; I am from above. You are of this world; I am not of this world. I told you that you would die in your sins; if you do not believe that I am the one I claim to be, you will indeed die in your sins.' 'Who are you?' they asked. 'Just what I have been claiming all along,' Jesus replied... They did not understand that he was telling them about his Father. So Jesus said, 'When you have lifted up the Son of Man, then you will know that I am the one I claim to be and that I do nothing on my own but speak just what the Father has taught me. The one who sent me is with me; he has not left me alone, for I always do what pleases him.' Even as he spoke, many put their faith in him.

The NIV puts brackets around 'the one I claim to be' to indicate that these words are not in the original text (vv. 24, 28): Jesus only says, 'I am'. At this point in the conversation, the authorities seem to miss Jesus' use of the name of God as he is describing himself, but there are others in the crowd who understand enough to make a decision. Jesus, the light of the world, sees clearly while those who dwell in darkness do not, but there are those who see enough to make a leap of faith and accept Jesus as the Messiah.

If we look back over the past 2000 years, we shall find times and places when the light of Christ seemed to shine so brightly that huge numbers of people responded. At other times and in other places it seems as though only a few saw the truth about Jesus. The same is true today. Why that should be is something of a mystery. Why is Christ's light being seen so clearly by so many in some countries and not in others? There are countless theories and only one truthful answer: because it is!

Whether people respond to Jesus in large numbers or in ones and twos, one thing remains constant. Jesus' words can sound like gobbledygook, until we make that leap of faith. Then Jesus makes perfect sense.

Prayer

Speak, Lord, I am listening.

DR

Slaves or free?

To the Jews who had believed him, Jesus said, 'If you hold to my teaching, you are really my disciples. Then you will know the truth, and the truth will set you free.' They answered him, 'We are Abraham's descendants and have never been slaves of anyone. How can you say that we shall be set free?' Jesus replied, 'I tell you the truth, everyone who sins is a slave to sin. Now a slave has no permanent place in the family, but a son belongs to it for ever. So if the Son sets you free, you will be free indeed.'

For these people to say, 'We are Abraham's descendants and have never been slaves' is ridiculous. Their ancestors were slaves in Egypt, their forebears were subjugated by various empires and they themselves were at that time ruled by Rome. In addition, it was by no means uncommon for some people in their culture to seek a way out of poverty by selling themselves (or family members) into slavery (Deuteronomy 15:12–18). For them to connect descent from Abraham with complete freedom was to rewrite their history, their culture—and their religion.

Passover was all about the journey from slavery to freedom and so was the Feast of Tabernacles. Abraham was the father of their faith, but Moses set the context (freedom, law, priesthood, sacrifice and worship, the journey, the land) and these formed the bedrock of Judaism. When Jesus told them here that 'everyone who sins is a slave to sin', he was not telling them anything new; their history was intertwined with slavery. When Jesus said, 'If the Son sets you free, you will be free indeed', however, he *was* saying something new. Until Jesus, the people looked back to freedom under Moses and looked forward to freedom from sin under the Messiah. They no longer needed to look back and forth: if they looked to Jesus the freedom that they longed for would be theirs.

As we come towards the end of John 8, the different strands of Jesus' teaching weave together. He is the bread of life, the living water, the light of the world. If we believe in him, put our faith in him, then his journey into death brings us freedom.

Prayer

Lord, without you I am a slave, but you set me free.

DR

Jesus: I am

The Jews answered him, 'Aren't we right in saying that you are a Samaritan and demon-possessed?' 'I am not possessed by a demon,' said Jesus, 'but I honour my Father and you dishonour me... Your father Abraham rejoiced at the thought of seeing my day; he saw it and was glad.' 'You are not yet fifty years old,' the Jews said to him, 'and you have seen Abraham!' 'I tell you the truth,' Jesus answered, 'before Abraham was born, I am!' At this, they picked up stones to stone him, but Jesus hid himself, slipping away from the temple grounds.

The people, baffled by Jesus yet again, try to silence him. First of all, they suggest that he is a Samaritan and, therefore, not a pure Jew. If that is true, he is a foreigner, not the Messiah, and can be safely ignored. Jesus doesn't even bother to answer this racist insult.

Second, they try to explain away Jesus' teaching and miracles by suggesting that he is possessed. What he says and does is clearly spiritual in origin, but if his power is evil, then he can, again, be ignored. Jesus confronts this accusation, saying that his teaching and miracles honour his father but what they say dishonours both the word and work of God. Also, if these people cannot discern the presence of God among them, how can they find the freedom Jesus offers?

Finally, Jesus speaks clearly about who he is and uses the name of God ('I am') about himself. This provokes their third reaction, which is to pick up stones to kill him, but Jesus slips away.

When he performs miracles, do the people see the sign or see where it is pointing? When Jesus teaches, do they hear a man or God? When Jesus speaks plainly, do they accept or reject him? The choice is always the same. He is either who he says he is—the Messiah whose miracles confirm his words—or he is... well, what? A man to be argued with, insulted, rejected and, ultimately, put to death. Yet this becomes the greatest sign of all as, in his death, he offers freedom and life to everyone. John, in his Gospel asks us, 'Do you *see*?'

Prayer
Lord, thank you that I see enough to put my faith in you.

DR

The BRF

Magazine

Richard Fisher writes...

I wonder what comes to mind when you think of Christian spirituality. Do you consider yourself to be on a spiritual journey? Is spirituality something that you associate with monks, nuns or saints rather than with yourself, or with places like a retreat house or monastery rather than where you live? I suspect that many of us wish we had a closer relationship with God, a better prayer life. We look at others and think, 'They seem to be so much better at this than I am.'

'Resourcing your spiritual journey' is what BRF's ministry is all about. We're passionate about making a deeper Christian spirituality more accessible for all of us. While some are called to the monastery or convent, we're all on a spiritual journey of our own, a journey that can lead us onwards towards God and deeper into a relationship with him.

Real spirituality finds God in the mundane and in all circumstances. Brother Lawrence discovered this as he peeled potatoes in the monastery kitchen; Jackie Pullinger discovered it among the drug addicts in Hong Kong. Recently my home group was talking about our experiences of prayer. One person needed silence to pray effectively; another said that they just fell asleep if they were sitting down in silence—they found they prayed best when they were out walking, doing something active. We're all different: one size doesn't fit everyone, and doesn't have to!

What can BRF offer to resource your spiritual journey? Our annual programme of Quiet Days offers a chance to step aside from the busyness of life and catch your breath. The *Quiet Spaces* journal provides articles, reflections and prayers, exploring a different theme each issue; and we continually add to our range of prayer and spirituality books. One to look out for this year is *The Circle of Love*, an accessible guide to one of the best-known and loved icons: Rublev's icon of the Trinity. *The Circle of Love*'s author, Ann Persson, a BRF trustees who regularly leads Quiet Days, writes about the book in this issue of *The BRF Magazine*.

Our prayer is that whoever you are, whatever your circumstances, Christian spirituality isn't something that you just recognise and admire in others, but an everyday experience of your own.

Richard Fisher, Chief Executive

The Circle of Love

Ann Persson

The Circle of Love
Praying with Rublev's Icon of the Trinity
Ann Persson

A few years ago I had an eye operation, after which I was required to lie face downwards for a fortnight. Instead of looking at the floor, which was very boring, I chose to have a print of Andrei Rublev's icon of the Trinity placed below me—so for two weeks the icon was my constant companion.

I found myself drawn in to the serenity and harmony of the three seated figures all blessing the cup of sacrifice on the table before them. The longer I gazed, the more engaged I became with the Father, the Son and the Holy Spirit and all that they represent. A potentially difficult experience had presented me with an unexpected gift.

A few months later I was asked to lead a four-day retreat for the Associates of St Mary's Convent, Wantage, and I used the icon as my theme, giving the retreat the title 'The Circle of Love'. Then I was asked to lead a Quiet Day and again I used the icon as my focus. Attending the Quiet Day was John Laister, husband of Karen, General Manager of BRF. He returned home to his wife with the suggestion that the material could be put into book form—and that is how the book came to be written.

It has given me a wonderful opportunity to find out more about iconography, of which I was quite ignorant—its history and the techniques of painting (purists would call it 'writing') icons. It has led to an exciting journey of discovery, central to which was a visit to Russia in the winter cold of January 2009. I went with a friend who is an icon painter, not only to see the icon that hangs in the Tretyakov Gallery in Moscow but also to visit the spectacularly beautiful monastery for which it was commissioned in 1425. This led me to delve into the remarkable life story of the hermit monk, St Sergius of Radonezh, around whom the

> *... the serenity and harmony of the three seated figures...*

monastery was founded and who is now the patron saint of Russia.

Rublev's icon is based on the story of the hospitality of Abraham as recorded in Genesis 18. In the story Abraham welcomes three travellers and has a meal prepared for them. However, halfway through the narrative, the visitors become as one and are called 'the Lord'. Iconographers were only allowed to depict Christ, the Son of God who became man. They were prohibited from depicting the Father and the Spirit, so they seized on this story as a symbol of the Trinity and of the hospitality that is not only Abraham's but is also at the heart of the Trinity.

The central part of the book is taken up with a long, slow look at the icon, which is rich in meaning. Icons are not intended to be objects of worship but, rather, aids to worshipping God. They are called 'windows on to the divine'. So it is not surprising that my journey took me into a further exploration of the doctrine of the Trinity, a concept that I, in company with many others, have never found easy to grasp. I was recently introduced to the theory of 'perichoresis' and this has helped me in my understanding. For more about it, read the book! There is a chapter on the invitation to us to become active participants in the life and love of God the Father, God the Son and God the Holy Spirit.

> ... a long, slow look at the icon

I am neither a scholar nor a theologian but I could describe myself as an enthusiast. I am delighted to have the privilege of serving as a member of the BRF council, as I am excited by the initiatives that the organisation is taking to resource the spiritual journeys of all age groups. I enjoy leading Quiet Days for BRF, as it gives me the opportunity to combine my love of God's word with my love of nature. In the pressured days in which we live, it is good to take breaks and give ourselves 'time out with God'. I find that I gain fresh insights and a larger perspective on my life, as well as deepening my relationship with God.

My hope is that the book will serve as a useful resource for anyone who might want to spend some quiet time and would appreciate a theme to work with. At the end of each chapter I have written suggestions for reflection.

It has been a huge privilege to write this book and I am grateful to BRF for commissioning it and to Andrei Rublev for his magnificent icon, but above all to the Trinity who invite me into the circle of love.

To order a copy of this book, please turn to the order form on page 159.

Becoming a more confident Christian

Foundations21
THE NEW WAY TO DO DISCIPLESHIP

Gilly Beardmore

Having used *Foundations21* for over three years, it's wonderful to look back and acknowledge its impact on my life. When I began to use the material, I was able to explore and investigate a lifelong faith in a new, refreshing and invigorating way, which now involves me in a closer relationship with God. This free website has become a routine and flexible tool for discipleship, one that I can rely on to support my Christian journey whenever I need it.

Foundations21 helped me to appreciate the Christian opportunities that God gives us in ordinary daily life. It broke down the temptation to put elements of faith in the separate boxes that are church, prayer, study, work and family. Now, instead, these threads are woven together, revealing God's purpose with a clearer focus. After taking the 'Learning quiz', I was directed to a 'gospel pathway' that best suited my personality and style of learning. I began to travel on a well-signposted journey through the various 'rooms'. Activities encouraged personal reflection; the development of strategies for prayer and Bible study; an acquaintance with key writers, past and present; the investigation and appreciation of diverse forms of worship, spending quality time with God; and an increasing awareness of Christian expression through the ages and into the 21st century.

Instead of being a passive Christian, I gained confidence in expressing faith wherever the need arose and in a variety of ways. I was encouraged, through the contents of the website, to review my Christian life. As a result, faith grew stronger and became a more urgent call on my time. Speed of reaction, materialism, consumerism, image and celebrity, the celebration of the individual at the expense of social justice, and the need to place blame and personal rights before responsibilities—the pressures of today's culture gradually faded in their impact and were replaced with the framework of support that was *Foundations21*. I was gently, patiently and at my own speed invited to examine my relationships with those individuals and groups who were part of my daily life, so that I came to know the blessings of new kinds of fellowship with

Christians and non-Christians whose paths crossed mine. I began to understand more sympathetically the pressures of our culture and how best to express and share the peace that God's love gives us all within it.

Foundations21 also raised an important personal question about the place of humble service. I had to learn to confront humility routinely. I am gradually learning its everyday characteristics through a more patient style of listening prayer—more than I ever did or could before. I now try to listen to God's will and increasingly question my motives before I make choices and decisions. I no longer rely on my own judgment and am more likely to sound out my husband, who is a fellow Christian, and other Christian friends. All these changes have been prompted by *Foundations21*.

I realise that each day invites me to a practical walk with God, which is not always easy and has many unpredictable twists, turns, ups and downs. *Foundations21* is helping me to act in response to opportunities I am given by the Lord. This may involve drafting a list of things to do after listening to the needs of others, or specifically setting aside time to read or pray. I find that I am now more aware of our personal call as stewards of God's creation and, as a result, am trying to improve our household recycling and energy use. Fair trade items appear in our shopping basket more often. I enjoy working in our Neighbourhood Watch alongside other neighbours and local community police support officers.

> *Foundations21... is a haven to return to...*

At church, I have been asked to be part of our Children's Church team. Recently, with a 17-year-old, I led a Lent course group and was also involved in another Lent course for children in our town. I have discovered the joy of sharing faith through writing. Before using *Foundations21*, I did not have the confidence to do any of these things and am now more appreciative of the importance of sharing talents and gifts with each other.

Foundations21 has undoubtedly enabled me to be a more confident Christian. It is something I can use very flexibly on a regular basis. It supports me in my attempts to discern God's purposes for my daily life and has enabled me to take part more fully in church, work and family life. It is a haven to return to when I need to say the Jesus Prayer, seek refreshment or simply know his loving presence.

Gilly Beardmore is a devoted user of Foundations21, *BRF's free web-based discipleship resource. To find out more about* Foundations21, *visit: www.foundations21.org.uk.*

Just as at the beginning

Martyn Payne

'Knowledge of the Bible and its stories is declining among people in the UK, according to a survey from St John's College, Durham University. The National Biblical Literacy Survey of people from faith and non-faith backgrounds revealed that as many as 60% could say nothing about the good Samaritan... 62% did not know the parable of the prodigal son... and only 20 interviewees were able to name all the Ten Commandments.' (Source: an internet news report in June 2009)

I wonder what your reaction is to the above paragraph? Incredulity? Sadness? Despair? Of course there are many reasons why this news might not come as a shock. There are large numbers of people in 21st-century Britain who have no contact with church and the Christian faith, so these people will not even be exposed to one or two Bible stories each week in church. There are some religious TV and radio programmes but they are often broadcast at times when few people are watching or listening. Then there are our schools. Contrary to popular Christian belief, Religious Education is still taught in schools, but Christianity is now only one faith among many. Indeed, the new Primary Curriculum guidelines may make it even harder for all but committed church schools to devote much time to exploring more than a few basic Bible stories.

So what is to be done? For the followers of Jesus, despair and resignation are not an option. Rather, this is an opportunity to tell our story with a new freshness—a freshness that might have begun to lose its edge in a more religious climate.

Barnabas Children's Ministry is the face-to-face work of BRF with children in churches and schools. I have been privileged to work with its team of gifted Bible storytellers for over six years now and with thousands of children up and down the country. One phrase from the story of Peter and the household of Cornelius in Acts 10—11 comes to my mind whenever I think back over this work.

When Peter eventually (and rather reluctantly) accepted Cornelius's invitation to preach the good news to a 'pagan' household, he saw the Holy Spirit fall on the Gentiles, just as it had on the first Jewish Christians at Pentecost. It was 'just as at the beginning', as he explains later to the elders back in Jerusalem (Acts 11:15). For us in the *Barnabas* team, telling the timeless stories of the Bible to a new generation of children, it is often 'just as at the beginning'. These are stories that the children have never heard before and our work, dare I say it, has the excitement that those first disciples of Jesus experienced as they set off from Israel to tell the stories of Jesus to the world of the first century AD. 'Just as at the beginning', we see children respond with enthusiasm and wide-eyed wonder as they hear about the people of the Bible who discovered that God made them, God loves them and God has a purpose of love for their lives.

Of course, *Barnabas* Children's Ministry is not alone in this endeavour to bring the Bible to life for the first time for 21st-century children. Like others, though, it has responded to the findings of surveys such as the one quoted at the beginning of this article, not merely as a crisis to bewail but as an opportunity to take.

These are stories that the children have never heard before

Because of your prayers, *Barnabas* Children's Ministry has become very widely known across the UK and is a much-respected part of the home mission work of the church—inspiring, supporting and adding value to the work done by local Christian teachers and children's leaders who share the same missionary zeal. Together we are responding to this opportunity, anxious to make sure that today's children do get to hear about the forgiveness of God as described in the story of the prodigal son, do become aware of the unchanging love of God and his commitment to us expressed in the Ten Commandments, and can respond to the world-changing challenge to love our neighbour with compassion, as expressed in the parable of the good Samaritan.

For more details about our *Barnabas* programmes and how we might work together with your local primary school and church, please get in touch with us by emailing barnabas@brf.org.uk. In this way, we, like the first Christians, can be among those who turn the world (and its surveys!) upside down.

Martyn Payne is a member of the Barnabas *children's ministry team, based in the south-east of England.*

Changes

Jane Butcher

Changes, changes! I imagine that many of us are aware of how things have changed over the years, whether that is in the context of the world, homes, churches or schools. Schools certainly have seen a number of changes, and those who have been teachers for a long time may be able to recall many that they have experienced.

However, one thing that seems to be fairly consistent in our work with Barnabas in Schools is the enthusiasm that children across the country show as they launch into the creative RE Days that we offer. During the course of a day, we often work with children across all of the primary school years from Reception (4 years old) to Year 6 (11 years old). While their responses can vary with their different ages and the location of their school—whether it be urban or rural—there still seems to be great excitement as they explore various themes from a Christian perspective.

Among the themes we offer are 'What's so special about the Bible?', 'Who is my neighbour?', 'Who am I?' and 'Whose world?' Each of the themes gives children a chance to consider the 'bigger picture' but also to explore the part they play in that picture. An important part of the day is allowing children to express their own thoughts, feelings and opinions without being told what to think.

RE Days are led either by a member of the Barnabas team—Martyn, Chris or Jane—or by our expanding team of freelancers. The freelancers are a gifted team of people across many areas of the country who also lead RE Days for us if the location or prior diary commitments mean that a team member is unable to cover them.

Those of us who lead the sessions discover new things alongside the children. It is always an important moment when a child shares something that he or she feels or has discovered, particularly if it arises from their own faith journey. This sharing is not something we expect of a child any more than we would expect it of an adult, but when it happens we feel privileged to be a part of it.

RE Days can be very tiring. They can involve an early morning start to travel to the school, a fairly intense day and often a tiring journey home (for some, contending with the challenges of London city traffic). That said, these times are important in allowing us a chance to share the Christian faith with children and staff, and we gain much, too. These days encourage and motivate us as well as allowing us to keep in touch with the lives of children and what is currently 'in' for them, and to hear about the joys and challenges that they face daily.

The role of RE in the curriculum may change

Another area of work within schools is INSET—a form of training that is offered to head teachers, staff teachers, classroom assistants and school governors. We can offer various training packages, including 'Using drama in RE', 'Storytelling and the Bible', 'Collective worship and reflection', 'Art and spirituality' and 'Using the Bible with children'. We can also lead 'Quiet Spaces', a time of retreat.

INSET sessions enable us to offer school staff some creative ways of delivering RE and assemblies, along with a large number of resources to assist them. We also gain the opportunity to see the world of education from the teachers' perspective and to encourage and support them in their roles, which may at times be the most valuable gift we can offer.

Things may change again quite significantly in the near future. The role of RE in the curriculum may change, which could also mean that we at Barnabas need to adapt our offering to the schools. We would value your prayers as we seek to stay in touch with everything happening in the world of education and to respond accordingly. We would also value your prayers for the days we spend in schools, and particularly for safety as we travel to and from them.

Please do pray for schools—the head teachers, class teachers and other staff who work in the school, whether in a paid or voluntary capacity, and for the pupils themselves. If your local school is close by, maybe you could pray as you walk or drive past. If you live further away, maybe you could set aside some time each week to pray for them.

Schools may be a place of change but they are exciting places where the lives of many children can be shaped and formed for this day and beyond.

Jane Butcher is a member of the Barnabas *children's ministry team, based in the Midlands. For information about RE Days and INSET, visit:* www.barnabasinschools.org.uk.

Recommended reading

Naomi Starkey

An important part of BRF's prayer and spirituality range are books reflecting the experiences of individual men and women. While books discussing in general terms how to pray or examining different strands of spirituality are helpful, many people find it equally helpful, if not more so, to hear how somebody gained a deeper understanding of God through their personal experiences.

The wilderness is an ancient and enduring symbol of the challenging times through which we may have to pass, just as the people of God did in Bible times. Lynne Chandler's *Embracing a Concrete Desert* shares an unfinished journey through both literal and figurative wilderness places. After moving with her family to Egypt, she spent weary months struggling to adapt to a very different environment. Her book shares her search for a path through struggle and difficulty to acceptance and peace of mind.

Despite the challenges of life in the teeming metropolis of Cairo, Lynne discovers how God can reveal fresh water springs for the soul in the driest of desert places. She realises, too, the importance of choosing to seek wholeness instead of clinging to heartache, and shares what she learns in a series of lyrical reflections and poems. With typical honesty, she writes:

I wish I could say that I have arrived and will never have to stare into the darkness again, but I know that isn't so. I do know, though, that I have to embrace the present moment and celebrate life, whatever that may involve today. My Creator is alive within and throughout this amazing world, and has never failed, through thick and thin, to wrap me in wings of protection and comfort. There are many layers of negativity to be peeled back so that a glimpse of God's image can show through. Just as one layer is lifting, another appears to take its place. That's where grace comes in. In desperate times, God dishes it out lavishly, like my grandma's generous servings of homemade strawberry shortcake.

A different but, at times, equally daunting journey is that of fatherhood. Brad Lincoln, author of *Six Men Encountering God* (BRF, 2008) has now written about what it means to be a dad to his three young children, and how that fits in with his feelings about life, the universe and God. *One Dad Encountering God* does not set out to provide all the answers but aims to get the reader thinking about what really matters.

For example, if we are made in the image of God, our heavenly Father, then presumably there is much we can learn about what it means to be a human father through looking at what God is like. At the same time, reflecting on our relationship with our own children can begin to open our eyes to how God feels about us. As Brad points out, God may have left an important clue about his personality somewhere inside us, as if, in making us, he left his signature. The book is designed so that it can be used as a month's worth of daily reflections for individual readers, but it also includes a section of material for group discussion.

As well as the seasons of life, the seasons of the Church's year, from Advent through Christmas, Easter, Pentecost and on to Advent again, can provide us with a helpful path, leading to personal growth and connection with the rich heritage of Christian history. *Seasons of the Spirit* takes us not only through the four seasons of the year but also through the high days and holy days of the liturgical calendar.

Interweaving poetry and prose, author Teresa Morgan draws on her experiences of ministry and worship in the parish of Littlemore, on the edge of Oxford, to share her sense of how God's love reaches out to transform the world. There are days of encouragement and rejoicing; there are also times when the walk of faith is a weary one. As she writes:

'Watch and pray.' Advent's motto is good for Lent, too. But I am too tired to pray; even the short step into silence seems a marathon. I am tempted to sit down under the chestnut tree and hope that the new life which touches it one sunny morning will quicken me too... We both know and can't know that Easter will come.

In his foreword for *Seasons of the Spirit*, Bishop John Pritchard describes it as 'wise and generous... accessible and full of insight'.

All three of these books offer moving insights into the joys and sorrows of the Christian life as lived by three individuals in very contrasting circumstances. They are books to read thoughtfully and prayerfully, asking God to reveal what we can learn from them to inspire us in our own discipleship pilgrimage.

To order a copy of any of these books, please use the order form on page 159.

An extract from *Working from a Place of Rest*

Working from a place of rest

Jesus and the key to sustaining ministry

Tony Horsfall

Exhaustion is all too common these days, not least among those involved in some kind of Christian ministry. We can easily forget that there were many times when Jesus himself was willing to rest, to do nothing except wait for the Spirit's prompting, so that he demonstrated the principle of 'working from a place of rest'. Drawing on extensive experience as a mentor, author Tony Horsfall reflects on the story of Jesus and the Samaritan woman to draw out practical guidance for sustainable Christian life and work. In the extract below, you can read the Introduction to the book.

One of the amazing things about the Bible is that you can be reading a familiar passage and suddenly the words seem to leap off the page and hit you between the eyes. All at once the significance of what you are reading bursts unexpectedly into your consciousness, and you become aware that God is speaking to you in a profound way.

It is rather like one of those grand firework displays. There is a bang, a burst of light, and coloured stars begin shooting in all directions. Then another, and another, until the whole sky is lit up. All you can do is stand back and watch in amazement. So it is with these moments of revelation, of spiritual illumination, of knowing something you never knew before. Your eyes are opened to a truth that was previously hidden; that which was obscure becomes plain; and it is not something you are making happen. It is the work of the Holy Spirit, taking the truth of God and making it known to you through the words of scripture. As one truth dawns, another opens up before you in the incredible unfolding process of spiritual awareness.

> *As one truth dawns, another opens up before you*

I enjoyed one such moment some years ago when I was reading

through John chapter 4. I came to the passage in the course of a reading scheme I was following at the time, and I arrived there with little expectation, having read the story of the woman at the well many times before. I was not expecting to receive anything new, merely to be reminded of familiar truths. Then I came to verse 6, and the fireworks began: 'Jacob's well was there, and Jesus, tired as he was from the journey, sat down by the well. It was about the sixth hour.'

In a flash I saw the tremendous significance of these simple words and realised something quite staggering in its implications. *Jesus was doing nothing.* He was having a rest, taking a break, giving himself a breather. Sitting there on the edge of the well, he was pausing and giving himself permission to stop and simply to be.

Then, just as quickly, the thought came to me that *everything that happens in this story happens because Jesus was doing nothing*. The fact that he is resting, taking some time out, is what gives him the opportunity to 'waste' time with the Samaritan woman who comes to the well while he is sitting there. Because of that life-giving conversation, not only is her life changed but the whole Samaritan town experiences revival. None of this is premeditated or planned. It is a purely spontaneous event, dependent on the fact that Jesus is doing nothing.

> *Christian ministry need not be a matter of striving to make things happen*

While I was still trying to get my head around this second insight, a third suddenly arrived. *We can learn to work and minister as Jesus did, from a place of rest.* Christian ministry need not be a matter of striving to make things happen or of straining to achieve our goals through the sweat of our brow. We can learn to work together with God just as Jesus did, for this was no idle moment; rather, it was a moment of communion, of sensing what the Father was doing and of responding accordingly. We can learn to co-labour with God, to collaborate with his Spirit and work in a way that is both efficient and effective. The work is not ours; it is his. If we slow down and take time to listen, he will guide us so that we can share in what he is doing. We can learn to live, to work and to minister to others from a place of resting in God.

I continued to ponder this verse over the next few weeks and months, and to develop my thoughts around the five headings you will find in this book. I have road-tested the material many times in seminars and retreats, and there has always been a good response. People seem to recognise this as something they already knew deep down inside but perhaps did not dare articulate. I continue to read around the subject to gain a broader understanding and I am continually reflecting on my own experience in the light of what I am sharing here, to see if it really does work. I think it does. I offer my thoughts to you with the prayer that they may liberate you into a healthier and more fruitful way of serving God.

The Evangelical Alliance (an umbrella organisation for many churches and organisations in the United Kingdom) met in September 2008 to address what it called a 'crisis in leadership' in the church in Britain. As well as an ageing leadership and a lack of emerging younger leaders, it noted that there is a depletion of leaders, because many drop out through exhaustion and depression.

Listen to what the Spirit may be saying to you deep within

This certainly concurs with my own observations. It is my privilege to work with church leaders, missionaries and key lay people in different parts of the world. 'Exhaustion' is a common word used, and 'tiredness' a number one problem for many. 'Burn-out' is something we are familiar with as a potential threat and, for some, a personal reality. I do not claim to have all the answers and I still struggle myself in some of these areas, but I believe that learning to work and minister in the way that Jesus did must be part of the answer.

So come and sit by the well for a while. Take some time out to reflect on how you are living and working. Watch Jesus and see how he does it. Listen to what the Spirit may be saying to you deep within, at the centre of your being; and maybe, just maybe, God will give you some insights that will change your life and sustain your ministry over the long haul.

Tony Horsfall is a freelance trainer and retreat leader, whose work regularly takes him around the world. He has also written Mentoring for Spiritual Growth *(2008) and* A Fruitful Life *(2006) for BRF. To order a copy of any of these books, please turn to the order form on page 159.*

Tony also leads Quiet Days for BRF. Information about these can be found at www.quietspaces.org.uk.

New Daylight © BRF 2010

The Bible Reading Fellowship
15 The Chambers, Vineyard, Abingdon OX14 3FE
Tel: 01865 319700; Fax: 01865 319701
E-mail: enquiries@brf.org.uk; Website: www.brf.org.uk

ISBN 978 1 84101 552 1

Distributed in Australia by Willow Connection, PO Box 288, Brookvale, NSW 2100.
Tel: 02 9948 3957; Fax: 02 9948 8153;
E-mail: info@willowconnection.com.au
Available also from all good Christian bookshops in Australia.
For individual and group subscriptions in Australia:
Mrs Rosemary Morrall, PO Box W35, Wanniassa, ACT 2903.

Distributed in New Zealand by Scripture Union Wholesale, PO Box 760, Wellington
Tel: 04 385 0421; Fax: 04 384 3990; E-mail: suwholesale@clear.net.nz

Publications distributed to more than 60 countries

Acknowledgments

As a Christian charity, BRF is involved in five distinct yet complementary areas.

- **BRF** (www.brf.org.uk) resources adults for their spiritual journey through Bible reading notes, books, and a programme of quiet days and teaching days. BRF also provides the infrastructure that supports our other four specialist ministries.
- **Foundations21** (www.foundations21.org.uk) provides flexible and innovative ways for individuals and groups to explore their Christian faith and discipleship through a multimedia internet-based resource.
- **Messy Church**, led by Lucy Moore (www.messychurch.org.uk), enables churches all over the UK (and increasingly abroad) to reach children and adults beyond the fringes of the church .
- **Barnabas in Churches** (www.barnabasinchurches.org.uk) helps churches to support, resource and develop their children's ministry with the under-11s more effectively .
- **Barnabas in Schools** (www.barnabasinschools.org.uk) enables primary school children and teachers to explore Christianity creatively and bring the Bible alive within RE and Collective Worship.

At the heart of BRF's ministry is a desire to equip adults and children for Christian living—helping them to read and understand the Bible, to explore prayer and to grow as disciples of Jesus. We need your help to make a real impact on the local church, local schools and the wider community.

- You could support BRF's ministry with a donation or standing order (using the response form overleaf).
- You could consider making a bequest to BRF in your will.
- You could encourage your church to support BRF as part of your church's giving to home mission—perhaps focusing on a specific area of our ministry, or a particular member of our Barnabas team.
- Most important of all, you could support BRF with your prayers.

If you would like to discuss how a specific gift or bequest could be used in the development of our ministry, Chief Executive Richard Fisher would be delighted to talk further with you, either on the telephone or in person. Please let us know if you would like him to contact you.

Whatever you can do or give, we thank you for your support.

BRF MINISTRY APPEAL RESPONSE FORM

Name _____

Address _____

_____ Postcode _____

Telephone _____ Email _____
(tick as appropriate)

Gift Aid Declaration

❏ I am a UK taxpayer. I want BRF to treat as Gift Aid Donations all donations I make from 6 April 2000 until I notify you otherwise.

Signature _____ Date _____

❏ I would like to support BRF's ministry with a regular donation by standing order (please complete the Banker's Order below).

Standing Order – Banker's Order

To the Manager, Name of Bank/Building Society

Address _____

_____ Postcode _____

Sort Code _____ Account Name _____

Account No _____

Please pay Royal Bank of Scotland plc, Drummonds, 49 Charing Cross,
London SW1A 2DX (Sort Code 16-00-38), for the account of BRF A/C No. 00774151

The sum of _____ pounds on ___ /___ /___ (insert date your standing order starts) and thereafter the same amount on the same day of each month until further notice.

Signature _____ Date _____

Single donation

❏ I enclose my cheque/credit card/Switch card details for a donation of
£5 £10 £25 £50 £100 £250 (other) £ _____ to support BRF's ministry

Credit/Switch card no. ☐☐☐☐ ☐☐☐☐ ☐☐☐☐ ☐☐☐☐ ☐☐☐☐

Expires ☐☐☐☐ Security code ☐☐☐ Issue no. (Switch card only) ☐☐☐☐

Signature _____ Date _____
(Where appropriate, on receipt of your donation, we will send you a Gift Aid form)

❏ Please send me information about making a bequest to BRF in my will.

Please detach and send this completed form to: Richard Fisher, BRF,
15 The Chambers, Vineyard, Abingdon OX14 3FE. BRF is a Registered Charity (No.233280)

ND 0210

An updated pack of resources and ideas to help to promote Bible reading in your church is available from BRF. The pack, which will be of use at any time during the year (but especially for Bible Sunday in October), includes sample readings from BRF's Bible reading notes and The People's Bible Commentary, and lots of ideas for promoting Bible reading in your church.

Unless you specify the month in which you would like the pack sent, we will send it immediately on receipt of your order. The pack is free if despatched to a UK address (but if you would like to make a donation towards the cost, we will greatly appreciate it). If you require a pack sent outside the UK, please contact us and we will quote for postage and packing. We welcome your comments about the contents of the pack and your ideas for future ones.

This coupon should be sent to:

BRF
15 The Chambers
Vineyard
Abingdon
OX14 3FE

Name _____

Address _____

_____

_____ Postcode _____

Telephone _____

Email _____

Please send me _____ Bible Reading Resources Pack(s)

Please send the pack now/ in _____ (month).

I enclose a donation for £ _____ towards the cost of the pack.

BRF is a Registered Charity

❏ Please send me a Bible reading resources pack
❏ I would like to take out a subscription myself (complete your name and address details only once)
❏ I would like to give a gift subscription (please complete both name and address sections below)

Your name _____

Your address _____

_____ Postcode _____

Tel _____ Email _____

Gift subscription name _____

Gift subscription address _____

_____ Postcode _____

Gift message (20 words max.) _____

Please send *New Daylight* beginning with the September 2010 / January / May 2011 issue: (delete as applicable)

(please tick box)	UK	SURFACE	AIR MAIL
NEW DAYLIGHT	❏ £14.40	❏ £15.90	❏ £19.20
NEW DAYLIGHT 3-year sub	❏ £36.00		
NEW DAYLIGHT DELUXE	❏ £18.00	❏ £22.50	❏ £28.80
NEW DAYLIGHT daily email only	❏ £12.00 (UK and overseas)		
NEW DAYLIGHT email + printed	❏ £23.40	❏ £24.90	❏ £28.20

Confirm your email address _____

Please complete the payment details below and send, with appropriate payment, to: **BRF, 15 The Chambers, Vineyard, Abingdon OX14 3FE.**

Total enclosed £ _____ (cheques should be made payable to 'BRF')

Please charge my Visa ❏ Mastercard ❏ Switch card ❏ with £ _____

Card number ☐☐☐☐☐☐☐☐☐☐☐☐☐☐☐☐☐☐☐

Expires ☐☐☐☐ Security code ☐☐☐ Issue no (Switch only) ☐☐☐☐

Signature (essential if paying by credit/Switch) _____

BRF PUBLICATIONS ORDER FORM

Please ensure that you complete and send off both sides of this order form.
Please send me the following book(s):

		Quantity	Price	Total
686 3	Embracing a Concrete Desert (L.E. Chandler)	_____	£5.99	_____
710 5	Seasons of the Spirit (T. Morgan)	_____	£5.99	_____
750 1	The Circle of Love (A. Persson)	_____	£5.99	_____
678 8	One Dad Encountering God (B. Lincoln)	_____	£6.99	_____
528 6	Six Men Encountering God (B. Lincoln)	_____	£6.99	_____
544 6	Working from a Place of Rest (T. Horsfall)	_____	£6.99	_____
562 0	Mentoring for Spiritual Growth (T. Horsfall)	_____	£7.99	_____
335 0	A Fruitful Life (T. Horsfall)	_____	£6.99	_____
708 2	The Barnabas Read-Aloud Bible (M. Wang)	_____	£9.99	_____
526 2	The Barnabas Children's Bible (R. Davies)	_____	£12.99	_____
707 5	The Barnabas Classic Children's Bible (R. Davies)	_____	£11.99	_____
530 9	My First Bible (L. Lane)	_____	£6.99	_____
046 5	PBC: Mark (D. France)	_____	£8.99	_____
118 9	PBC: 1 & 2 Kings (S.B. Dawes)	_____	£7.99	_____
071 7	PBC: Proverbs (E.B. Mellor)	_____	£7.99	_____
047 2	PBC: Ephesians to Colossians and Philemon (M. Maxwell)	_____	£7.99	_____

Total cost of books £ _____

Donation £ _____

Postage and packing £ _____

TOTAL £ _____

POSTAGE AND PACKING CHARGES				
order value	UK	Europe	Surface	Air Mail
£7.00 & under	£1.25	£3.00	£3.50	£5.50
£7.01–£30.00	£2.25	£5.50	£6.50	£10.00
Over £30.00	free	prices on request		

For more information about new books and special offers, visit www.brfonline.org.uk.

See over for payment details.

All prices are correct at time of going to press, are subject to the prevailing rate of VAT
and may be subject to change without prior warning.

PAYMENT DETAILS

Please complete the payment details below and send with appropriate payment and completed order form to:

BRF, 15 The Chambers, Vineyard,
Abingdon OX14 3FE

Name _____

Address _____

_____ Postcode _____

Telephone _____

Email _____

Total enclosed £ _____ (cheques should be made payable to 'BRF')

Please charge my Visa ❏ Mastercard ❏ Switch card ❏ with £_____

Card number: ⬚⬚⬚⬚⬚⬚⬚⬚⬚⬚⬚⬚⬚⬚⬚⬚⬚⬚⬚⬚

Expires: ⬚⬚⬚⬚ Security code ⬚⬚⬚ Issue no (Switch only): ⬚⬚⬚⬚

Signature (essential if paying by credit/Switch) _____

❏ Please do not send me further information about BRF publications.

ALTERNATIVE WAYS TO ORDER

Christian bookshops: All good Christian bookshops stock BRF publications. For your nearest stockist, please contact BRF.

Telephone: The BRF office is open between 09.15 and 17.30. To place your order, phone 01865 319700; fax 01865 319701.

Web: Visit www.brf.org.uk

ND 0210

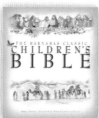
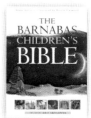

New Daylight provides four months of daily Bible readings and comment, with a regular team of contributors drawn from a range of church backgrounds. It is ideal for anybody wanting an accessible yet stimulating aid to spending time with God each day, deepening their faith and their knowledge of Scripture.

Rooted in the rhythms of the Christian year, New Daylight is published in January, May and September and covers a varied selection of Old and New Testament, biblical themes, characters and seasonal readings. Each day offers a short Bible passage (text included), thought-provoking comment and a prayer or point for reflection. Also included, The BRF Magazine highlights the wider ministry of BRF and Barnabas, with articles, book extracts and information on our funding and prayer needs.

Also available from BRF

Guidelines

Guidelines offers in-depth study and comment, covering biblical books and themes. The daily readings are arranged in weekly sections, each including an introduction and points for thought and prayer.

Readers' comments on New Daylight:

'I have always found the daily readings to be a very important part of my journey through life.'

'The daily notes are sometimes challenging and offer spiritual and prayerful reflection.'

'Please thank all your writers. We feel as if we know each one personally.'

'Many thanks for making the Bible more accessible for us all.'

New Daylight is also available in other formats: deluxe, Braille, and on cassette for the visually impaired. For more information see page 2.

978-1-84101-552-1
UK £3.80

9 781841 015521

visit the **brf** website at www.brf.org.uk

Photograph: Photolibrary.com

Design: Louise Blackmore/ Christine Reissland